Bible Fun

FOR AGES 11-14

How's Your Serve?

David C Cook
transforming lives together

HOW'S YOUR SERVE?
Published by David C. Cook
4050 Lee Vance View
Colorado Springs, CO 80918 U.S.A.

David C. Cook Distribution Canada
55 Woodslee Avenue, Paris, Ontario, Canada N3L 3E5

David C. Cook U.K., Kingsway Communications
Eastbourne, East Sussex BN23 6NT, England

Written by Cheri Gillard
Cover Design by BMB Design/Scott Johnson
Interior Design by TrueBlue Design/Sandy Flewelling
Illustrations by Marilee Harrald-Pilz, Trapdoor Media

Scripture quotations, unless otherwise noted, are taken from the HOLY
BIBLE NEW INTERNATIONAL VERSION®. Copyright © 1973,
1978, 1984 by International Bible Society. Used by permission of
Zondervan. All rights reserved.

ISBN 978-1-4347-6716-5

First Printing 2009
Printed in the United States

1 2 3 4 5 6 7 8 9 10

TABLE OF CONTENTS

INTRODUCTION

Kids in middle school or junior high are in a crucial—and often difficult—time of development. They've heard things from their parents and teachers all their lives and are ready to begin testing those concepts, putting legs on biblical truths and lessons. The service projects in this resource help you lead the way to successful and effective application of God's instructions. The activities will empower your youth to develop the autonomy they need to implement their faith, and to think for themselves in new ways that build and strengthen that faith.

Kids in this age bracket vary widely in maturity, social skills, independence, and spirituality. While some are "12 going on 20," others may be content to interact with peers in "typical" middle-school fashion (if there even is such a thing), while still others will continue to desire the security of close parental contact. Spiritually, these students may be ready to explore incredibly deep ideas about God and theological questions about life and Scripture. And others may simply parrot back cliché answers they've picked up over the years.

No doubt, working with this age group has challenging moments. So a strong, united group of leaders is essential. Your team needs to be spiritually stable and mature, as well as able to connect with and relate to middle schoolers. Utilize your volunteer helpers. Gather around you other support to not only help you face the many challenges, but to provide a good, effective ratio of adults or older teens to kids.

Working with kids in this age group can be the most rewarding thing you've ever done. To see God's hand move in the lives of these impressionable youth, and to know you have a partnership with the Spirit to lead them on the path toward the Lord, is a privilege and challenge like no other.

May you rely on the Lord to equip you well, and may He give you strength and endurance to accomplish the exciting work He has in store for you!

HOW TO USE THIS BOOK

The 26 activities in this book can be done in any order and easily fit into any curriculum. Simply use the Scripture and Topic Index on page 110 to match a project with the lesson you're teaching. These activities also can be used as alternate Step Three activities in several curriculum lines: David C. Cook Bible-in-Life, Echoes, LifeLINKS to God, College Press, Reformation Press, Wesley, Anglican, and The Cross. If you have one of these lines, look through the Correlation Chart on page 111 and find the activity geared to your lesson. You'll use this new activity instead of one of the other Step Three activities listed in your teacher's guide. This book, when combined with *Design and Devour*, will give you a full year's worth of Step Three replacement activities for the middle-school age group.

A brief explanation of each project appears after the Bible Background to explain what the project entails. The goals of the project follow. The Teacher Tips with each service project will help you know how to better enable your students to enjoy the project. Many of the projects are completed during normal meeting time. Some partly will take place outside of class time, utilizing the class time to plan or prepare for the later event. Some include options that describe ways to do the same project either in class or outside of class. Debriefing questions at the end of each project may be used in class to prepare or after the entire project is completed as follow-up to promote discussion and contemplation.

And It Was Very Good

Plant crocus bulbs to showcase God's beautiful creation.

BIBLE BASIS:
Genesis 1:26–28; 2:7

MEMORY VERSE:

I praise you because I am fearfully and wonderfully made; your works are wonderful, I know that full well.
Psalm 139:14

BIBLE BACKGROUND

When you feel special, what is it that makes you feel that way? Is it the way you look? Is it something you've accomplished? Is it because someone tells you that you're special?

God's Word teaches that each of us is special. It has nothing to do with our appearance, how we do in school, or the number of friends we have. In fact, it has nothing to do with *anything* we do. Rather, it has *everything* to do with who God made us to be.

When God created people, He made us different than all the rest of His creation. He made us in His own image—a reflection, in some mysterious way—of God Himself. Because God made us in His image, we can think, reason, and respond to God through relationship. Our reflection of God's image is one of the reasons He values us more than all other created things. Sometimes we need to remind ourselves of this and to help others know God also made them in His image.

We can use the abilities He gave us to share with others how much God loves and values them. As we serve others with our talents, God's love will flow through us, and those we are serving will realize how much God cares for them. As you will see, even something as simple as planting flowers can display God's love for His creation. We can then use that creation to show others how much God loves them.

Always remember that the God of the universe made you special. You are fearfully and wonderfully made above everything else in His creation. As beautiful as the flowers are that you will plant for this activity, you are many times more beautiful to God. And there is nothing anyone can ever do to take your beauty or value away, because they were given to you by God Himself.

PROJECT

Students will plant crocus bulbs outdoors in a designated area where beautiful flowers can pop up in the spring. If unable to plant outside, bulbs may be planted in pots.

GOALS

- To help students recognize how much God loves and values us because we are made in His image

- To help students understand that they are God's prized creation

- To use one of God's beautiful creations to let others know how much God cares for them

TEACHER'S TIPS

Crocus flowers are a delight in the spring, showing their glorious heads of color before the rest of creation awakens from its winter slumber. If permission can be obtained to plant bulbs in a church lawn or other appropriate area, you'll have a beautiful show of color to enjoy next spring, giving witness to God's beautiful creation and His creative nature. Their small blooms will be gone before most lawns green up and not cause interference with mowing and other summer grass maintenance.

If you prefer, the bulbs can be "forced" by planting for indoor enjoyment. Plastic or terra-cotta pots will work well for growing the bulbs. If indoor containers are used, other flowering bulbs, such as tulips or hyacinths, can be substituted.

SUPPLY LIST

For outdoor planting:
- ☐ Crocus bulbs (at least 1 or 2 per student; more if area permits)
- ☐ Trowel or shovel

For indoor planting:
- ☐ Flower bulbs (1 or 2 per student)
- ☐ 4-inch pot (1 per student)
- ☐ Potting soil
- ☐ Water
- ☐ Colorful, blank index cards
- ☐ Ribbon
- ☐ Hole punch
- ☐ Markers

INSTRUCTIONS

For outdoor planting:

1. Prior to the activity, determine where the bulbs will be planted. Be sure to request permission if you are planting the bulbs on the church grounds. Take into consideration the location of sprinkler heads and any other special planting instructions.

2. Gather in the planting area with garden tools and bulbs.

3. Cut very small flaps in the sod with a shovel, and curl back for bulb placement beneath sod level.

4. Place bulbs beneath sod with root end down.

5. Replace flap of sod and tamp down with foot.

6. Repeat until all bulbs are planted in either a random or predetermined pattern.

7. Water sod flaps well.

8. If planting in a rocky or sandy area without sod, plant in similar manner, at about a 3-inch depth.

For indoor planting:

1. Place each pot in a saucer or inverted lid to catch water overflow. (Terra-cotta pots should come with saucers.)

2. Place a small amount of dirt in bottom of each pot.

3. Place a bulb, root-end down, in pot and cover with dirt.

4. Punch a hole in the corner of an index card.

5. Have the student think of one person (a neighbor, friend, teacher, or relative) to give the pot to. With that person in mind, have the student write a message on the card, such as the memory verse and a note about how that person is God's most beautiful and wonderful creation.

6. Tie the card around the pot.

7. Encourage the students to tell their recipients how they learned that, of all God's amazing creations, we are loved and valued the most. We are even more beautiful to Him than the flower that will bloom in their pot.

PROJECT WRAP-UP!

God made us in His image, giving us the ability to please Him through His creation by using the wonderful things He made to help others know and respond to Him.

- **How does planting flowers reflect God?** *(planting flowers is a picture of creating in that I can nurture something and help it grow, I can witness God's beauty and care in the flowers He's made, etc.)*

- **How can we communicate with God while planting flowers?** *(I can thank Him for creating me to be like Him with the ability to think, reason, speak, etc; I can praise Him for the beauty of all His creation; I can consider how God is like a gardener, nurturing me and helping me grow, etc.)*

- **What are some ways the flowers you planted might help others know about God and learn to have a relationship with Him?** *(they can see the beauty in His creation and realize how much care He gives to all of His creation; they can recognize that God has made them like Himself, and therefore values them and loves them; etc.)*

Best Friends Forever

Correspond with senior citizens.

BIBLE BASIS:
Genesis 2:18–23

MEMORY VERSE:
*A friend loves
at all times.*
Proverbs 17:17a

BIBLE BACKGROUND

God is a God of relationship. Even before He created people, He existed in a state of relationship. The Father, the Son, and the Holy Spirit together make up our amazing God in a mysterious way that's full of wonder. The three parts, or Trinity, are in relationship to one another while also being one triune God.

When God gathered all the creatures He just made for Adam to name, it became obvious that none was a satisfactory companion for Adam. Adam needed someone more like himself. He needed to have a relationship—or friendship—with another person.

God wanted Adam to have a partner, a helpmate, a friend. He put Adam into a deep sleep and removed one of his ribs, which He then formed into another human being. Adam called her Eve, which was a form of his own name, because she came from him. God had provided Adam with a special friend.

Just as God wanted Adam to have a suitable companion, He made each of us to have companions. We were not created to be alone. Friends are important, but they are not automatic. We need to be a good friend to have friends. Jesus showed us how to be a good friend. In the Book of John, Jesus taught there is no greater way to show a friend love than to give up your life for that friend. Jesus did just that. He died so we can have a relationship with God. That's how important such a friendship was to Him. He invites you, and every person, to be His BFF—His best friend forever!

PROJECT

Students will connect with a senior citizen through letter writing, providing a return envelope with a request to write back.

GOALS

- To allow students an opportunity to establish on-going relationships with seniors
- To help students value other generations
- To bless seniors with correspondence from a middle schooler

TEACHER'S TIPS

Senior citizens are a great source of special friendships for children. They often have many stories and experiences to share, more time than younger adults, and often a desire to pass on lessons learned from many years of living.

Help your students connect to a generation they may not typically have contact with, and at the same time, bring delight and meaning to others who may be lonely, bored, or just looking for personal interaction.

If your congregation has a population of seniors, approach them and organize a letter swap with those who would like to participate. If you need another source for elderly writing companions, contact a retirement community (start by working through the community's activities director) and arrange pen pals that way. Encourage students to continue writing to their new friends as a long-term activity.

SUPPLY LIST

- ☐ Note cards/stationery with envelopes (quantity needed is the number of whichever group—seniors or students—is greater)
- ☐ Pens and markers
- ☐ Extra #10 envelopes (1 per letter)
- ☐ Postage stamps (double the number of each letter sent)
- ☐ Index cards (1 per senior)
- ☐ Names and addresses of seniors

INSTRUCTIONS

1. Write each senior's name and contact information on an index card.

2. Give each student a card. Or, have students pull them from a bag or basket. If there are extras, distribute to students willing to write to more than one person. If too few, have more than one student write to the same person.

3. Hand out note cards or stationery, markers, and pens.

4. Explain to students they'll be exchanging letters with senior citizens. While not a requirement, encourage students to make this an on-going activity and to keep in touch with their senior pen pal long term. Prompt them to include the following in their letters:

   ■ Introduce yourself (age, grade, school, etc.).

   ■ Share what is important to you and what you enjoy doing.

   ■ Ask your pen pal what he or she enjoys and values.

   ■ Ask what the person enjoyed doing when he or she was your age.

   ■ Ask if there is anything they'd like kids your age to know.

   ■ Ask your pen pal to share about his or her family.

5. Encourage students to decorate their letters to showcase their individual creativity and style. Have them address their envelopes properly for U.S. Postal Service mailing or for hand delivery.

6. Give each student a stamped envelope. Instruct them to self-address an envelope, fold it, and include it in their letter.

7. Mail letters or deliver by hand. Hand delivery would offer a great way to begin a more personal relationship with their pen pals.

PROJECT WRAP-UP!

God made us for relationship with others. One way to fulfill that desire is to reach out to those we may not normally spend time with. God wants us to show others friendship and that we care for them.

- **Why is it important to care for others?** (*so I can show God's love, to help me not to be selfish, so I can help people when they're in need, etc.*)

- **What do you find difficult about making new friends, especially with people who are different than you?** (*finding something I can talk about with them, feeling uncomfortable, etc.*)

- **What do you think makes a good, loving friend?** (*listening well, helping when trouble comes, being a companion, being trustworthy and dependable, etc.*)

- **What can you do to be a good friend?** (*I can pay more attention to others, I can refuse to spread gossip, I can try to help others more, etc.*)

- **What kind of relationships do you have with senior citizens? What would you like to see come from a friendship with someone of an older generation?** (*Answers will vary.*)

Mercy Me

Labor for the needy.

BIBLE BASIS:
Genesis 4:1–16

MEMORY VERSE:
The LORD is compassionate and gracious, slow to anger, abounding in love.
Psalm 103:8

BIBLE BACKGROUND

Have you ever heard the phrase, "Am I my brother's keeper?" It's a commonly used phrase that comes from today's Scripture passage in Genesis 4. After Cain murdered his brother, Abel, God asked Cain where Abel was. Cain answered, "I don't know. Am I my brother's keeper?"

God didn't need to ask, of course. He knew what had happened—just like when Cain's parents ate the fruit from the forbidden tree in the Garden of Eden. They hid when they heard God coming. God asked, "Where are you?" to provide an opportunity for them to confess their sin and restore their relationship with Him. He offered this same chance to Cain.

But just like his parents, Cain tried to cover up his sin. He tried to mislead God and not take responsibility for what he had done.

The most amazing thing about the story of Cain killing his brother is the mercy God showed him. There were indeed consequences for the murder, but in the midst of those consequences, God protected Cain. He forbade anyone from killing him. If anyone did, that person would "suffer vengeance seven times over."

God loved Cain, even though he killed his brother and lied to God. Consider your own life and your sin. Know that no matter how you live or what you do, God is merciful to you because He loves you. And His love covers a multitude of sins. Because of God's great mercy toward us, we are able (and responsible) to show mercy to others.

PROJECT

Students will determine who has a need they can address and then meet on a given date to work to accomplish the task.

GOALS

- To show mercy to others by offering and supplying physical labor
- To bless others in need
- To help others see God's love and mercy in action

TEACHER'S TIPS

Allow your middle-school students the opportunity to explore and develop how they want to use their abilities and energy to help others. Provide guidelines to keep them on track, but keep them loose and flexible so students have a chance to discover how they can contribute to and experience the deep satisfaction of making a difference in someone's life.

Ahead of time, prepare some names and possible projects. Ask your pastor or deacons who would benefit from help. Or ask around your congregation for names of neighbors who are in need, such as the elderly, struggling families, widows, or single parents.

Ask the students how they want to offer their services and whom they would like to help. Consider an announcement in a bulletin or church service, or pass out fliers in your church neighborhood. Make a plan for organizing the recipients and the workday (by whom, how, and when each task will be accomplished).

Emphasize that the project is not to get the recipients to start coming to your church or even to create a chance to tell them about God. Let them understand that being merciful means there are no strings attached, no expectations, and no agendas. When Jesus told us to love others, He didn't say to love others so we could get them to attend our church. It is to show God's love. Sometimes that's all we're supposed to do.

SUPPLY LIST

For planning in class:

- ☐ Paper and pens
- ☐ Church directory or list of possible service recipients

For the service project day:

- ☐ Any tools necessary for specific work, such as rakes and cleaning supplies
- ☐ Snacks and beverages for break time and to share
- ☐ Games or food to use at gathering after the work is done

INSTRUCTIONS

In class, you will plan your workday. Then you will meet another time, outside of class, to have your actual workday. Consider the following as you plan your project:

1. What kind of projects can you offer? Raking leaves, weeding, or other yard clean up; house cleaning; babysitting; and garden maintenance are all possibe ways to help others.

2. How will you arrange your workforce? Will you all meet as one team and work together, or will you break into smaller groups, work for more than one person, and gather when the work is through for a meal or game?

3. When you are finished, how can you build a relationship with those you helped? Should someone bring snacks to share with them? Can you invite them to participate with you at your gathering afterwards?

On the workday:

1. Meet at a pre-planned location, and go to the work site together.

2. Take any necessary equipment to accomplish the work.

3. Work well together as a team. Stay on task and do a thorough job, as though you are doing the work for Jesus Christ Himself (because, ultimately, you are!). Have fun as you work, but save playtime for your gathering afterwards.

4. Clean up any supplies or a work area that you've made untidy.

5. Gather for fun and food, celebrate helping others, and have a great time!

PROJECT WRAP-UP!

God shows us His mercy. Lamentations 3:23 tells us His mercies are new every morning. He shows us mercy and love, and He wants us to do the same for others.

- **How have you shown mercy and love to others in the past?** *(I've shown patience, I've forgiven others, I've given second—or third, or fourth—chances, etc.)*

- **How has someone else shown you mercy, and how did you respond?** *(Answers will vary.)*

- **Why do you think God showed mercy to Cain even after he killed his brother and lied about it?** *(it is God's nature to show mercy, because He loved Cain so much, because He wants to bless His creation, etc.)*

- **What would you like to see as a result of doing work for a stranger or needy person?** *(the person will be relieved of a burden, the person will know someone cares, the person will know God loves them, etc.)*

- **How can you show mercy in new ways?** *(Answers will vary.)*

I've Fallen, and I Can't Get Up

Explore humility and act it out by cleaning up trash.

BIBLE BASIS:
Genesis 11:1–9

MEMORY VERSE:
Pride goes before destruction, a haughty spirit before a fall.
Proverbs 16:18

BIBLE BACKGROUND

After the Flood, God told Noah and his sons to "be fruitful and increase in number and fill the earth." Many years later, when the people moved eastward, they decided they didn't want to scatter anymore. They wanted to stay in one place and make a name for themselves. They were puffed up with pride and wished to do as they pleased.

They planned to build a tower, one that would reach to the heavens. But God would not have it. It was an act of defiance against Him. God confused their language, making it impossible for them to communicate and thereby continue their plan to become a great people on their own. The building project stopped, and the people scattered. Their plans couldn't stand up against God and His intentions for the world.

The Bible teaches that pride is a sin. Pride is reliance on yourself when you should rely on God. Pride is trying to be the god of your own life. The Bible also teaches that pride will result in destruction and failure.

Once you fall, who will lift you back up? Through the process of destruction and failure, you might learn that being your own god isn't all it's cracked up to be. You can't save yourself. Only God can truly save you.

So when you've fallen and can't get back up, rely on God to pick you up, restore you to life, teach you to be humble, and help you to keep Him as the Lord of your life.

PROJECT

Students will explore the meaning of humility and practice it by cleaning up trash in a public area.

GOALS

- To help students recognize how they view humility
- To allow students an opportunity to humble themselves
- To clean an area of your community for the benefit of all

TEACHER'S TIPS

Middle-school students are certainly aware of appearance, both in their apparel and actions. It might be difficult for some to give up their perceptions about picking up trash or cleaning other people's messes. Help them understand what humility means. Explore with them their feelings (and perhaps your own) about humility, how Jesus showed humility, and things in our culture that fight against humility.

As you explore together what humility looks like, use a dictionary and thesaurus to find words associated with humility. Divide the words into two groups—those with positive and negative connotations. Discuss which words represent humility to each student. Discuss other, new ways of perceiving humility. Help the students understand that subtle beliefs can affect how they behave, how they treat others, and how they desire to be treated.

SUPPLY LIST

For planning in class:

- ☐ Dictionary, thesaurus, or printouts from the Internet containing definitions and synonyms of *humble* and *humility*
- ☐ Paper and pens

For the service project day:

- ☐ Any tools necessary for specific work, such as gloves, trash bags, buckets, or reach extenders/pick sticks
- ☐ Water and beverages as needed
- ☐ Any safety gear required, such as orange vests if visibility is an issue (check with local authorities, and choose a project with low safety risks)
- ☐ Chaperones

INSTRUCTIONS

Choose an area to clean that is in obvious need, would benefit the community, and can be safely cleaned up by removing small items of trash and debris.

1. Meet at the pre-arranged location and time.

2. Distribute any necessary supplies, such as vests, trash bags, water, or gloves.

3. Proceed to area of cleanup.

4. Break into teams or small groups and divide the area to be cleaned.

5. Encourage students to find ways to make the work enjoyable, such as singing as they clean, challenges against the clock or other teams, or making up stories about how certain pieces of trash ended up where they are found.

6. Take regular water breaks.

7. Have additional areas designated for cleaning in the event your work takes less time than anticipated.

8. Dispose of collected trash appropriately when finished.

PROJECT WRAP-UP!

One way to keep control of our pride is by serving others. We may avoid serving others because it is humbling, and society doesn't always teach us to value serving. But God teaches us to serve. He teaches that the first will be last, and the last will be first. Jesus washed the feet—the dirty, road-worn feet—of His disciples. That wasn't something a king would do. But He did, and He wants us to do the same.

- **How did the people of Babel show pride?** *(they disobeyed God, they wanted to be well-known, they wanted to do their own thing without regard to what God wanted, etc.)*

- **Share an example of how pride resulted in failure in yourself or someone you know.** *(Answers will vary.)*

- **What new things have you discovered about your perception of humility from this activity?** *(Answers will vary.)*

- **How did you feel about picking up the garbage? Did it reveal anything to you about pride in you?** *(Answers will vary.)*

- **If not cleaning up trash, what would be a challenge for you to do because of pride?** *(Answers will vary.)*

- **How does pride keep you from doing what is right?** *(I don't want to look dumb or un-cool, I want to do my own thing, etc.)*

- **What can you do to let go of pride and become more humble?** *(I can give up control to God, I can stop trying to be something God doesn't want me to be, etc.)*

A Penny for Our Pots?

Make pots and collect change for a good cause.

BIBLE BASIS:
Genesis 14:14—15:1

MEMORY VERSE:
*You cannot serve both God and Money.
Luke 16:13c*

BIBLE BACKGROUND

Abram was very intentional about the stewardship of his wealth. He provides a godly example for us to follow regarding the management of our own money and possessions. Consider what he did and what that might say to us today.

Abram soundly defeated Kedorlaomer and the kings allied with him. He reclaimed their captives (including his nephew Lot), retrieved the spoils that had been seized, and drove the enemy far from the area. Abram and his 318 men did what four kings and their armies could not. God was with Abram in a mighty way.

Abram returned victorious, and the king of Sodom—one of the defeated kings—came out to meet him. At the same time, Melchizedek, king of Salem (later called Jerusalem), brought out bread and wine. Melchizedek gave Abram a blessing and acknowledged God the Most High as the one who delivered Abram's enemies into his hands.

In response, Abram gave a tenth of all he had to Melchizedek.

The king of Sodom told Abram to keep all the spoils brought back and to only return the reclaimed captives. But Abram refused his offer to keep the plunder. He didn't want the king of Sodom to be able to claim any credit for what God would do for Abram. Abram wouldn't even accept a "thong of a sandal" from him.

What do Abram's actions show us? Not only are we to give back to God a portion of our possessions in order to show our dependence on Him, and acknowledge He is the source of our provision, but we are to be careful about the sources from which we receive profit. Are you accumulating and disbursing your possessions in a way that is honoring God? Consider how you spend your money. What have you purchased in the last week or month? And during that same time, how have you used your money or possessions to honor God?

PROJECT

Each student will make a pot to take home and fill with pocket change over a determined amount of time. The combined amount in the pots will then be donated to a cause of the students' choosing. The students may fill their pots with their own change or solicit contributions from others.

GOALS

- To help students recognize their perspective on money
- To allow students an opportunity to intentionally use their money to bless others
- To encourage students to depend on God as their source of provision

TEACHER'S TIPS

Keep in mind the wide range of budgets present among your students as you proceed with this project. Some will have a regular allowance or other source of income while others may have no source of income. The incomes will vary dramatically, from pocket change to amounts you may find baffling compared to your own childhood experience.

Steer away from discussions that might lead to revelation or comparison of students' income or wealth. Instead, keep the emphasis on the recipients and the heart with which gifts should be given. Also, planning the activity to focus on collecting loose change will allow everyone to participate equally.

SUPPLY LIST

- ☐ 3-inch terra-cotta pot (1 per student)
- ☐ 3 ½-inch terra-cotta pot saucer (1 per student)
- ☐ Acrylic paint in a wide variety of colors
- ☐ Art foam (if pots have holes in the bottom)
- ☐ Scissors (for cutting art foam)
- ☐ Damp rags
- ☐ Paint brushes
- ☐ Permanent markers
- ☐ Acrylic, clear-spray coating

do ahead Have available several options of charities from which students can choose. Then when it's time to decorate their pots, they will have a recipient to name on their pots to make it more personal.

INSTRUCTIONS

1. Determine a recipient for the proceeds earned from the project. Consider special needs in your congregation or designated ministry funds promoted and collected by regional or denominational affiliations. Agencies serving impoverished children may also suit your students' interests.

2. Distribute a pot and saucer to each student. Invert saucer and use as a lid.

3. Wipe pot and saucer with a damp rag to clean. Let dry.

4. Paint pot and lid. Decorate as desired. Using permanent marker over dry paint, include a message within the decoration stating the memory verse, the name of the recipient, or the project's purpose.

5. Trace the bottom of the pot onto art foam. Cut out circle, cutting on the inside of the line by 1/8 inch, then place in the bottom of the pot to cover the hole.

6. Spray the pot and lid with clear coat. (Spray outside or in a well-ventilated, open area.)

7. Take home and fill with change. Return by designated date and donate to pre-determined recipient.

PROJECT WRAP-UP!

The best way to show we don't hold on too tightly to money is to let go of it and pass it on to someone else. By doing so, we show we trust God to provide for us and bless others at the same time.

- **When do you find it difficult to give away your money or possessions?** *(when I don't have much, when I've worked hard to get it, when I don't know exactly where it's going, etc.)*

- **Why do you think it's difficult for you?** *(I need to control where it goes, I like my money, I want to spend my money on myself, etc.)*

- **When is it easiest for you to be generous?** *(when it's for someone I like, when I know I'll get something in return, when I pray and ask God to help me, etc.)*

- **Share a time you were blessed by someone's generosity.** *(Answers may vary.)*

- **What can you do to become more generous and more willing to give up your possessions?** *(give some away every time I get some, sponsor an orphan and support him or her regularly, ask God to help me be generous, etc.)*

- **What new thoughts have you had about giving up money while preparing this project?** *(Answers will vary.)*

Trust in Him

Serve a meal to the needy in your community.

BIBLE BASIS:
Genesis 22:1–12

MEMORY VERSE:
Love the LORD your God with all your heart and with all your soul and with all your strength.
Deuteronomy 6:5

BIBLE BACKGROUND

Think of something you've always wanted more than anything else. Something you've had to wait and wait for. Something like nothing else you've ever had.

Abraham had something like that. It was a son. God had promised Abraham a son when he was 75 years old, but it wasn't until he was 100 years old that he and his wife had a son, Isaac.

Now think again of that something you've always wanted. What if you got it, enjoyed it for a while, cherished it, loved it— but then you were told you had to give it up? And what if you weren't given a reason? You just were commanded to destroy it. How would you feel?

When God told Abraham to take his son on the journey to Moriah, He didn't give any explanation. He only said that Abraham was to sacrifice Isaac. When God told him to do so, He even acknowledged Isaac as someone very dear to Abraham. He said, "Take your son, your only son, Isaac, whom you love, and go to the region of Moriah." But God made no promise to rescue Isaac at the last minute. He gave no hint that everything would be okay.

Abraham had to take a step of faith. He was about to get thrown into a very uncomfortable and frightening circumstance. But God had proved Himself faithful to Abraham before. Abraham knew He could trust God to make a way. His faith showed when he told his servants to wait while he and Isaac go worship and then "*we* will come back." He also proved his trust in God when Isaac asked him where the sacrifice was for worshiping, and Abraham replied, "God himself will provide the lamb."

Abraham had no idea how God was going to do it, but he knew He would make things work out, even if it meant raising Isaac from the dead. When you find yourself in uncomfortable or even scary circumstances, know that you can trust God to see you through. You don't have to know how He'll do it; just know that He will.

PROJECT

Students will co-labor with a local soup kitchen, shelter, or rescue mission to serve a meal to a group of people with whom they are not normally in contact.

GOALS

- To allow students to step out of their comfort zones to serve others
- To allow students to depend on God in circumstances that may be uncomfortable and challenging
- To teach students to trust in God in a new way

TEACHER'S TIPS

Check with local organizations to arrange a meal that your students can serve. Consider a Thanksgiving meal, allowing the students an opportunity to give service when they would normally be in the familiar homes of family or friends, or around a time of abundance in their own lives, so they can consider in a new way the contrast with those in need. If a Thanksgiving meal is not possible, arrange another time to serve a meal to the needy in your community or within the network of local churches.

Confirm age requirements and chaperone needs with the organization you choose to work with. Enlist students' parents to participate with them in the meal, providing the entire family with an opportunity to help others together.

SUPPLY LIST

- ☐ A local shelter or soup kitchen that serves meals to indigent or needy individuals
- ☐ Contact person to help make arrangements, meet you at your arrival, and guide the group through the event
- ☐ Information to aid in communicating with and understanding those with whom you will have contact

INSTRUCTIONS

For preparation in class:

1. Determine where and when you will be serving.

2. Arrange the meeting place and transportation details.

3. Invite others to participate, such as siblings and parents.

4. Discuss how serving and/or eating a meal with people who are needy, and perhaps homeless, might be quite uncomfortable and will require the students to depend on God's help.

5. Talk about various situations you may encounter to help prepare those who are new to serving in this type of environment.

For the day of serving:

1. Pray to prepare your heart. Ask God to help you trust Him when you encounter new people and perhaps uncomfortable circumstances.

2. Depend on God as you serve others.

3. Make time after the project to debrief, sharing thoughts and experiences with one another.

PROJECT WRAP-UP!

Like Abraham, we sometimes face situations that are uncomfortable, unpredictable, and perhaps even frightening. But God has shown that He is dependable and trustworthy.

- Do you believe God is trustworthy? If so, why? *(He says so in the Bible, I've experienced it, etc.)*

- When do you find it easiest to trust God? *(after I've seen Him do things in my life, when things are going well, etc.)*

- When is it the hardest for you to trust Him? *(when things are tough, when I'm scared, etc.)*

- How would you respond if God asked you to give up something you cherish for Him? *(Answers will vary.)*

- Discuss a time you gave up something for God. *(Answers will vary.)*

- What do you do when you find yourself in uncomfortable, unpredictable, or frightening circumstances? *(pray, freak out, worry, trust God, etc.)*

Would I Lie to You?

Prepare meals for the ill or needy in your congregation.

BIBLE BASIS:
Genesis 29:13–30;
31:38–45, 51–53

MEMORY VERSE:
*The LORD detests lying lips, but he delights in men who are truthful.
Proverbs 12:22*

BIBLE BACKGROUND

Deceit brings heartache and ruins relationships. Jacob's lies destroyed his relationship with his parents, his brother, and also his uncle.

Jacob had to flee for his life from his brother, Esau. He had deceitfully snatched the blessing of his father that rightfully belonged to Esau. Jacob escaped to his uncle Laban's home. There, Jacob fell in love with Laban's daughter Rachel and made a deal with Laban to work for him for seven years in trade for Rachel's hand in marriage.

When the time came for Jacob and Rachel to marry, Laban deceived Jacob and tricked him into marrying Rachel's older sister, Leah, instead. Jacob convinced Laban to let him marry Rachel, too, but Jacob would have to work another seven years.

Jacob stayed and worked for Laban a total of twenty years. But it wasn't easy.

Those years were filled with difficulty and strife. The deceit Jacob had practiced against his own father and brother came back to haunt him when Laban deceived him over and over again. Jacob reaped what he had sown.

When Jacob and his uncle finally parted ways, it was not on good terms. They drew a boundary between them and swore never to cross it. They would forever be separated.

Had Jacob and Laban worked on building trust with each other, their story would've been quite different. We must keep our promises and work at developing trust with others if we want to build and maintain strong relationships.

PROJECT

Students will prepare meals for ill or needy members of your congregation.

GOALS

- To allow students an opportunity to build relationships and gain trust with congregation members

- To provide meals to those in need or who are ill

- To have the ill or needy be blessed through your students' service

TEACHER'S TIPS

Help students build relationships and develop trust with other members of the congregation by caring for their needs and showing that they keep their promises. Determine how many meals your class can prepare, then arrange to share the meals with those in your congregation who may be needy or sick. Use the recipes provided or any of your own that would be easy to prepare in the classroom.

Encourage students to use their meal as an opportunity to begin developing relationships with the beneficiaries. This shouldn't be a one-time blessing but rather something that is used to bring the students' closer to members of your church. Stress the importance of delivering meals when they say they will in order to begin building trust with those receiving meals.

SUPPLY LIST

For each group have available:

- ☐ Disposable (foil) 9" x 13" baking dish
- ☐ Food service gloves
- ☐ Recipe ingredients (see recipes)
- ☐ Can opener
- ☐ Bowl
- ☐ Spoon
- ☐ Foil
- ☐ Permanent marker
- ☐ Non-stick food spray

INSTRUCTIONS

1. Break class into groups.

2. Prepare a clean work area.

3. Wash hands well and don gloves.

4. Follow recipes and assemble meals. Cover with foil.

5. Write cooking or other preparation instructions with marker on foil covering.

6. Deliver to recipient.

Chicken Enchiladas

- one 10-oz. can chicken
- two 10-oz. cans mild enchilada sauce (one can could be thick and chunky)
- one 8-oz. package shredded cheddar cheese
- one 16-oz. can refried beans
- 1 small can sliced black olives
- 8 flour tortillas

Mix the beans, chunky enchilada sauce, chicken and ¾ of the cheese in a bowl. Spoon the mixture into tortilla, roll or fold closed, and place in dish. Repeat with remaining tortillas. Pour the second can of sauce over all tortillas, coating well. Sprinkle the remaining cheese and black olives over top. Cover with foil sprayed with non-stick food spray. Bake 20 minutes at 350 degrees.

Spinach and Sausage Cannelloni

- one 10-oz. package chopped spinach, thawed and drained
- one 16-oz. carton ricotta cheese
- one 8-oz. package shredded mozzarella cheese
- 4-oz. shredded parmesan cheese
- one 9 to 10-oz. box precooked, frozen Italian breakfast sausage patties, thawed and broken into pieces
- one 8-oz. box manicotti/cannelloni pasta noodles
- 1 jar Italian pasta sauce (at least 24 ounces)

Combine cheeses (except half of mozzarella), spinach, and sausage in bowl. Pour ½ of sauce in thin layer on bottom of dish. Stuff mixture into uncooked pasta shells with gloved fingers or small spoon. Place filled shells in dish. Cover completely with remaining sauce, then remaining mozzarella. Cover with foil sprayed with non-stick food spray. Bake one hour at 350 degrees. Uncover and bake another 15 minutes.

PROJECT WRAP-UP!

Relationships are important to God. Having good relationships requires honesty and hard work. They don't just happen on their own.

- **Think about your relationships. Share about one that was harmed by dishonesty.** *(Answers may vary.)*

- **Share about one that was built by keeping promises.** *(Answers may vary.)*

- **How do you feel when you find out someone you care about has been dishonest with you?** *(I feel hurt, I feel betrayed, I feel like maybe they don't really care about me, etc.)*

- **How do you feel when you know someone's gone to great lengths to keep their promises to you?** *(I feel like that person really cares about me, I feel that the person knows it's important to keep their word, etc.)*

- **Why do you think God detests lying?** *(God is truth, Satan is a liar, falsehoods put up barriers in relationships, etc.)*

- **What can you do to keep the promises you make?** *(ask for God's help, don't make promises I know I may not be able to keep, be very careful what I promise people, etc.)*

Piece of Peace

Collect books for young children and spend time reading with them.

BIBLE BASIS:
Genesis 45:1–11

MEMORY VERSE:
*Let the peace of Christ rule in your hearts, since as members of one body you were called to peace. And be thankful.
Colossians 3:15*

BIBLE BACKGROUND

Joseph had good cause to be angry with his brothers. And they knew it. They were terrified when they found out that Joseph was not only alive, but that he was the very ruler of Egypt standing before them with authority to do with them whatever he wished.

But instead of exerting his authority, Joseph chose to forgive them and not stay angry. He recognized that God allowed all that had happened to him so he would be positioned to take care of his family when they needed it most.

Because he had forgiven his brothers, the bondage of hatred and fear was broken. Joseph was free to weep with overwhelming emotion when he saw them. He could send a word of blessing back to his father. He could promise to take care of his family in the difficult years ahead.

Because Joseph let God's peace rule in his heart, he could pass that peace onto others. If Joseph had refused to let God's peace rule in his heart, he wouldn't have been able to bring his family to Egypt to care for them and rescue them. The promise God had made to Abraham to make his descendants into a great nation wouldn't have been fulfilled as it was. But Joseph did let God rule in his heart, therefore God was able to use Joseph's experiences to help others.

PROJECT

Students will collect books for young readers, read with the children, and then let them keep the books.

GOALS

- To allow students to use their personal experiences to help others
- To help younger children learn to read and enjoy reading more

TEACHER'S TIPS

Young readers sometimes love to read out loud but other times feel overwhelmed with the challenge. Encourage your students to be sensitive to the needs and desires of the child with whom they read. Use the opportunity not only to show the children what fun reading can be, but also to provide a chance for them to practice reading.

SUPPLY LIST

- ☐ Age-appropriate, value-based books for young readers

do ahead

• Ask each student to bring a favorite book for young readers (new or in good condition) to read and ultimately keep. Be sure to choose books that are age-appropriate and portray biblical values.

• Consider involving your congregation by asking for donations to provide increased options for books.

• Try to find a group of youngsters who may not normally have opportunities for reading time with others or who may not enjoy reading. Networking through your church's mid-week children's programs or school-teachers who are part of your congregation may help you locate such children.

• Consider an on-going relationship and reading time over the course of several weeks.

INSTRUCTIONS

1. Arrange a time with parents or teachers of youngsters to have your students read with their children.

2. Have each student bring a favorite book for a young reader.

3. Teach students how to read out loud with their child. Coach them on how to be expressive, enthusiastic, and encouraging.

4. Have each student pair up with one child and spread out throughout the room.

5. Read together. Allow the children to read words or phrases they know. Read the story aloud with plenty of expression and enthusiasm. Involve the children in the process by asking questions about the story and pictures as you go.

PROJECT WRAP-UP!

God wants us to use our own experiences to help others. In fact, sometimes He teaches us specific lessons through the hard things we experience so we'll be better able to help others with what we've learned.

- **In what ways have others helped you as they've drawn from their own experiences?** *(Answers may vary.)*

- **What's an experience you've had that allowed you to help someone later?** *(Answers may vary.)*

- **How were you able to help?** *(I could help a friend have hope, I knew what not to say because I didn't like when it was said to me, etc.)*

- **What is something unique and special about yourself that you can use to help others?** *(Answers will vary—help students recognize something positive and good about themselves.)*

- **In what ways can you help a younger child when you read with him or her?** *(I'm a very good storyteller, and I can make reading fun; I've never been a good reader, and I know how hard or embarrassing it can be to read out loud; etc.)*

... But He Is Strong

Create coupons for acts of service to give to others.

BIBLE BASIS:
Jeremiah 1:1–7; 7:1–7

MEMORY VERSE:
All Scripture is God-breathed and is useful for teaching, rebuking, correcting and training in righteousness, so that the man of God may be thoroughly equipped for every good work. 2 Timothy 3:16–17

BIBLE BACKGROUND

Do you ever feel insignificant or consider yourself too inexperienced to be able to do something important for God's kingdom? When you look around at others in your church, maybe you feel like there's no way you can do a good enough job to impact the world for the amazing God of the universe. Perhaps you think God would never expect you to act when all those other people—seemingly better people, smarter people, more experienced people—are available.

Remember the song, "Jesus Loves Me"? The words say, "Little ones to Him belong; they are weak, but He is strong." Paul the apostle wrote about his own weaknesses in 2 Corinthians 12. He said it is because of his weaknesses that Jesus Christ can be strong in him. If we could be completely capable without God's help, then God would not get the glory when something mighty is accomplished. God intentionally uses the small, frail, or ill-equipped for His work.

Repeatedly in the Bible, God does this to show His power. For example, when Gideon was to fight the Midianites, God told him he had too many men, and if they all fought and beat the enemy, Israel could boast they did it themselves. So God had Gideon send home over 32,000 men, and only 300 stayed and conquered the Midianites. They knew God's strength had defeated the enemy, not their own. And, of course, there is the story of David and Goliath. And the small boy with the fish and bread. Jesus used his small lunch to feed over 5,000 people.

The next time you think you're insignificant or too inexperienced to impact the world for God, think again. He just needs someone who is willing to trust Him and obedient to follow Him. He'll do the rest!

PROJECT

Students will make coupons to offer service to others, utilizing their abilities to help with housework, yard work, childcare, pet care, etc.

GOALS

- To allow students the opportunity to impact others, especially in areas where they may have little confidence
- To bless others by providing practical help

TEACHER'S TIPS

Help your students explore the various ways they are uniquely gifted and how they can apply those abilities toward helping others. Ask them what types of things they feel they do well and what areas others have noticed they have a talent in. Once students have identified some of the gifts and talents God has equipped them with, give them examples of service ideas that make use of those gifts and talents. Help them to brainstorm how they can serve others with their unique gifts.

Then, go further and challenge them. Help them think of areas in which they might not necessarily believe they have skills or feel equipped or strong. Encourage them to stretch themselves by providing a service using these gifts, trusting that God will use their efforts for His good, enabling and strengthening as He sees fit.

SUPPLY LIST

- ☐ Paper
- ☐ Markers
- ☐ Scissors
- ☐ Staplers

INSTRUCTIONS

1. Choose ways you will serve others and what kind of coupons you will create.

2. Cut paper to desired coupon size.

3. Design your coupons, including on them the conditions of the service.

4. Coupons may all be given to the same person or distributed to a number of people.

5. Stapling them together may help students keep track of their coupons.

GOOD FOR (1) BABYSITTING SESSION UP TO 3 HOURS

PROJECT WRAP-UP!

God gives us what we need to do His work. It's even better when we go into a situation feeling insecure or weak, because it allows God to work in and through our lives and to showcase His strength.

- **How have you used your strengths to serve God?** *(I'm outgoing and I can make others feel comfortable, I'm artistic and create cards/gifts for others, etc.)*

- **What are some of your weaknesses where you may be uncomfortable or afraid to serve others?** *(being in front of large groups, talking out loud, meeting new people, being around sick people, etc.)*

- **In what ways could God use your weakness to show His strength?** *(He can give me the right words to say, He can help me accomplish a tough chore if it will bless someone else, etc.)*

- **What are some things in God's Word, specifically about serving others, that you find a challenge to obey?** *(taking care of the poor, encouraging others when they're down, blessing my enemies, etc.)*

- **What have you done out of obedience to God even though you were uncomfortable or afraid?** *(Answers may vary.)*

- **Who can you make a coupon for, and what service can you offer, that will specifically use one of your weaknesses and allow God to show His strength through you?** *(Answers will vary.)*

Man Does Not Live by Cupcakes Alone

Have a bake sale.

BIBLE BASIS:
Matthew 4:1–11

MEMORY VERSE:
For we do not have a high priest who is unable to sympathize with our weaknesses, but we have one who has been tempted in every way, just as we are—yet was without sin.
Hebrews 4:15

BIBLE BACKGROUND

When someone says something you dislike or disagree with, it is so easy to come back with a quick response that pushes your own opinion or agenda. How much harder it is to hold back, to show respect, and allow the other person to have the last say. Especially if you just *know* you're right.

Oftentimes, resisting temptation feels really hard, like holding your tongue when your brother just said the most obnoxious thing to you that you can imagine. You just want to give up all restraint and let him have it.

But God wants us to resist temptation, just as Jesus did. When He was in the wilderness and Satan came to tempt Him, He was surely worn down, hungry, and lonely. He was vulnerable. But He didn't give in. He drew His strength from God. He used Scripture to fight off the temptations the devil put before him.

Because Jesus went through temptation—meaning He was invited or enticed to sin—He can understand what it is like for us to be tempted. Hebrews tells us Jesus has been tempted in every way we are. So He knows, too, that there is always a way out, a way to resist. James 4:7 says that if we resist the devil, he will flee.

So next time someone yanks your chain so hard you want to yank her chain right off, remember that though it is tough and doesn't always feel like what you want to do, try choosing the right thing. Practice resisting temptation. And see how good it feels, in the end, to have chosen to do what God wants you to do.

PROJECT

Your class will hold a bake sale to raise funds to support a worthy cause.

GOALS

- To raise funds to support a worthy cause
- To allow students an opportunity to choose a recipient and become more missional in their world view
- To encourage students to consider the deeper meaning of spiritual food, and how it prepares and equips them to resist temptation.

TEACHER'S TIPS

Consider including your entire church in the effort to gather baked goods. Invite those known for their baking prowess to make special donations of bread, cakes, pies, and/or pastries. Approach local bakeries to contribute to your sale, making the recipient of your efforts clear.

When pricing the items, use a master list to determine prices, rather than trying to price individual items. Also, state that prices are suggested donations, and anything additional would be greatly appreciated.

As you work with your students to prepare, emphasize that although you are selling baked goods such as bread, the underlying truth is that Jesus teaches that bread is secondary. The Word of God is what feeds us, making us strong to resist temptation.

 You may wish to apply your proceeds toward sending service-men and servicewomen letters and care pack-ages as suggested in —the upcoming project entitled, "Thank God!" found in this book.

SUPPLY LIST

- ☐ Fliers for advertising
- ☐ Tables
- ☐ Chairs
- ☐ Baked goods
- ☐ Plastic wrap or bags
- ☐ Cash box and change for paper currency
- ☐ Information on and/or picture of beneficiary

INSTRUCTIONS

In class, prior to the event:

1. Determine a beneficiary for funds raised.

2. Choose date, time, and place for event to take place.

3. Plan informational flier.

4. Assign someone to create fliers.

5. Determine when and how to distribute information about the sale.

6. Determine what baked goods are needed and who will supply what.

On the day of the event:

1. Set up tables and display goods in an attractive manner.

2. Place chairs on one side of the table for those collecting the money.

3. Display information about the beneficiary.

4. Encourage donations in addition to suggested prices.

PROJECT WRAP-UP!

Jesus knows all about temptation. And He also knows about resisting it. It isn't done through human strength but by depending on God and relying on His Word.

- **What kinds of things are hardest for you to resist when you are tempted to do wrong?** (*Answers will vary.*)

- **How do you respond when you are tempted?** (*I pray, I recite Scripture, I'm too overwhelmed to think straight, I don't notice until it's too late, etc.*)

- **What do Jesus' words, "Man does not live on bread alone ..." mean to you?** (*that we can trust God to care for our needs, it's important to read and learn from the Bible, etc.*)

- **How did Jesus resist temptation?** (*He used Bible verses to speak truth about the temptation, He didn't do what would be easy or comfortable, etc.*)

- **Share a time when you recognized you were tempted to sin but were able to stand strong and resist. How were you able to resist?** (*Answers will vary.*)

- **How do you feel when you've been able to resist temptation? How do you think God feels when you resist temptation?** (*Answers will vary.*)

- **How does knowing that Jesus was tempted in every possible way make it easier for you to resist temptation?** (*because I know He's made a way for me to resist, because I have the same power He does to overcome temptation, etc.*)

"BE MINE," Says Jesus

Make valentines and commit to help someone.

BIBLE BASIS:
Matthew 9:9–13

MEMORY VERSE:
By his power he may fulfill every good purpose of yours and every act prompted by your faith.
2 Thessalonians 1:11

BIBLE BACKGROUND

Schools have groups or cliques. Workplaces have them too. Pretty much anywhere you have people gathered for any length of time, they will migrate into smaller groupings, looking for others with whom they can relate or find some level of comfort.

Jesus broke through the barriers of the cliques and groups of His time. He didn't let what others thought keep Him from doing what He knew was right or what accomplished His purpose.

The tax collectors were a group of despised people. They used their position to take advantage of others. The Pharisees were another group. They were very secure in their position of power and prestige, and they looked down on everyone else.

When Jesus spent time with the despised people, the Pharisees criticized Him. They didn't understand why He'd spend time with *those* kinds of people. And they tried to make Jesus look bad for doing so.

The reason Jesus wanted to spend time with those people was because they were the ones who needed Him most. Jesus came to bring sinners into a relationship with Himself and with His heavenly Father. He wanted to reach out to these people and show them how much He loved them.

It's difficult to befriend those who are different from us. But as Christians, we need to reach out to all people, especially those who have been marginalized by others. By doing so we will display the love of Jesus and potentially bring them into a relationship with Him.

PROJECT

Each student will make a valentine with the intent of giving it to a specific person who is outside of the student's current social group. The valentine will include a commitment on the student's part to perform some act of service for the recipient.

GOALS

- To allow students the opportunity to pray to determine an act of service and a recipient to bless with the service

- To bless someone with an act of love or care

TEACHER'S TIPS

It's hard for some middle-schoolers to believe and understand that the Holy Spirit will prompt them to action and give them the equipping to fulfill that action.

Help them understand this truth by sharing personal examples of how God has led you and then equipped you to "... fulfill every good purpose of yours and every act prompted by your faith" (2 Thess. 1:11).

Encourage students to consider a recipient who may not be popular or who does not fit comfortably into most social circles. Tell them this is their chance to be like Jesus and show these types of people His love.

SUPPLY LIST

- ☐ Colored construction paper, including red, pink, and white
- ☐ Scissors
- ☐ Glue
- ☐ Stickers
- ☐ Envelopes

INSTRUCTIONS

1. Spend a few minutes in prayer and reflection. Ask God to bring to mind something He would like you to do for another person and to show you who that other person is.

2. Make a valentine for that person. Write on the valentine the act of service you would like to do.

3. Deliver the valentine.

4. Ask when a good time would be to complete your commitment or to create a plan to do so.

5. Follow through by doing what God has prompted you to do.

PROJECT WRAP-UP!

Jesus' main focus wasn't on people who thought they were already righteous. His message was for those who realized they needed to change, for sinners desiring forgiveness and redemption.

- ■ Describe a time when someone has reached out to you to do something nice for you. *(Answers may vary.)*

- ■ Describe a time when God helped you reach out to others. *(Answers may vary.)*

- ■ In what way has God helped you see your need to change? *(my conscience wouldn't let me keep doing what I was doing, He used a friend to tell me about a sin, etc.)*

- ■ What made you feel God prompted you to make the valentine that you made and for the person you made it for? *(Answers may vary.)*

- ■ What might be difficult about carrying out your valentine commitment? *(finding the time, being brave to approach the person, serving with the right attitude, etc.)*

Fast: Food

Meet during meal time, skip the food, and pray for others.

BIBLE BASIS:
Matthew 14:22–23a;
Mark 14:32–36;
Luke 6:12–16

MEMORY VERSE:
When you pray, go into your room, close the door and pray to your Father, who is unseen. Then your Father, who sees what is done in secret, will reward you. Matthew 6:6

BIBLE BACKGROUND

Jesus instructed us to pray privately, without the need to show off to others. He told us to not let anyone know when we fasted, hoping people will think we're super-spiritual. Our Father will know when we do these things, and He will reward us. Jesus' own example of praying shows us how important it was to Him to communicate with His Father.

He set aside time for prayer. He did this when He intentionally sent His disciples ahead and dismissed the crowds so He could go to the mountains to pray.

He separated Himself from people and distractions to have time alone with His Father. In the garden of Gethsemane before His arrest, although He took His disciples along for support and comfort, He went ahead of them to be alone before God the Father.

He allowed plenty of time for prayer. Before He chose and called the disciples to follow Him, He spent an entire night in prayer.

He used prayer to prepare for important tasks.

He depended on God for guidance, which He sought through prayer.

He spent time in prayer, ignoring the needs of His physical body to exercise spiritual discipline.

He shared His heartfelt desires and feelings through prayer.

He submitted His own will to the Father through prayer.

What does your prayer life look like? Does your schedule keep you too busy to pray? Do distractions keep you from really entering into authentic communion with God? Do you prepare for challenging circumstances through prayer? Consider how you might relate to God in a new and more real way by following the Lord's example as you spend time with your heavenly Father.

PROJECT

Students will meet together during a normal mealtime, forgoing the meal to pray for the needs of the church, Sunday school groups, and any others for whom they wish to pray. Then they will spend some time alone in prayer.

GOALS

- To spend time in intercessional prayer for the needs of others while skipping a meal
- To experience the discipline of fasting
- To practice spending time alone with God

TEACHER'S TIPS

Some students may not be comfortable praying out loud. Share with them that prayer doesn't have to look or sound any special way to "count." Help them understand that it is okay to talk to God as if speaking to a friend.

Some may be unfamiliar with the concept of fasting. Explain that fasting from food is a way to put more dependence and emphasis on God. Remind them of Jesus' words in Matthew 4:4 when He was tempted after forty days of fasting: "Man does not live on bread alone, but on every word that comes from the mouth of God."

Start your prayer time by inviting the class to share prayer concerns. If students are uncomfortable praying for a specific person, let them know they can just say that person's name. At that point, everyone can simply pray silently for that individual according to the prayer concern shared earlier.

Encourage students to use their time alone with God to pray for friends and family, to journal, and to sit quietly in the Lord's presence.

If a child has a medical issue, such as diabetes, that makes fasting a concern, encourage him or her to "fast" something else, such as video game time, and to spend that time in prayer.

variation If it doesn't work well to meet during a meal, use your normal meeting time and encourage the students to skip their next meal and continue in an attitude of prayer. Or if you usually share snacks during class time, choose to not have snacks to emphasize the idea of sacrifice and eliminating distractions for prayer.

SUPPLY LIST

- ☐ Bibles
- ☐ Paper
- ☐ Pens/pencils
- ☐ Quiet area

Inform your class ahead of time to be thinking about prayer concerns for others as well as for themselves.

INSTRUCTIONS

1. Read aloud Isaiah 58:6-12.

2. Share prayer concerns.

3. Take notes for reference.

4. Spend time in prayer for those in need among your church family, community, loved ones, and friends.

5. Split up and spend time alone with God.

PROJECT WRAP-UP!

Jesus knows how important it is for us to spend quality time with our heavenly Father. Because of this, He gave us a model from His own life of prayer to follow. Fasting is just one component of a strong prayer life.

■ **What was it like for you to give up a meal to spend time with God?** *(it was difficult to concentrate, it made me feel closer to God, it felt good to sacrifice for others, etc.)*

■ **How did it affect you to spend concentrated time praying for others?** *(I became more aware of God's presence, it made me less selfish, etc.)*

■ **What did you like best about spending the time alone in prayer?** *(I felt peaceful, it got me to look outside of myself, it helped me connect with God, etc.)*

■ **What can you do to meet with God more regularly?** *(set a time each day, have a designated place to pray, keep a journal, etc.)*

■ **If you journaled during your time alone with God, how did journaling help you pray?** *(it focused my thoughts, it kept those we were praying for in my thoughts, etc.)*

"In fasting, we are learning by experience that we do not 'live by bread alone, but by every word that proceeds from the mouth of God.' Any one who has ever experienced this reality knows that 'inward joys' is a good description."
—Richard Foster, *Celebration of Discipline*

A Can Can Cheer

Write messages of forgiveness on canned goods and deliver to a food pantry.

BIBLE BASIS:
Mark 2:1–12

MEMORY VERSE:
If we confess our sins, he is faithful and just and will forgive us our sins and purify us from all unrighteousness.
1 John 1:9

BIBLE BACKGROUND

The teachers of the law who watched as Jesus healed people didn't seem to have trouble believing God could forgive sins. Their problem was with Jesus offering forgiveness to those He healed. They didn't believe that Jesus was who He claimed to be—the Son of God, the expected, longed-for Messiah.

When Jesus healed a man whose friends had lowered him through a hole they'd torn in the roof, Jesus said, "Your sins are forgiven." The teachers of the law thought negatively about Jesus, like He was blaspheming God, which means to speak strongly or offensively about God.

Jesus knew what they were thinking, so He asked them why they had those thoughts. He knew they didn't believe in Him. But by proclaiming the man's sins were forgiven and by healing him and telling him to get up and walk, Jesus demonstrated that He was who He said He was—that He had authority and was God's Son. Even though the teachers wouldn't believe in Jesus, the crowds who were watching did, and they were amazed and praised God.

Do you believe Jesus has forgiven you? Do you truly believe He has the power to both forgive sins and heal? Thank Jesus that He has cleansed you from all of your unrighteousness and made a way for you to have a relationship with His Father. No sin is too big for Him to handle!

PROJECT

Students will bring canned goods, write messages of truth and the hope of Jesus' forgiveness on the cans, then donate them to a food pantry for distribution.

GOALS

- To allow students the chance to contemplate the meaning of forgiveness
- To express the truth of Jesus' forgiveness in messages for hurting people
- To provide food and messages of hope to the needy

TEACHER'S TIPS

Help students create encouraging messages that reflect God's forgiveness in short, clear phrases. Have several examples written ahead of time on a whiteboard or poster board. Also provide Bible references and a concordance so students can look up verses and include those of their choosing on their cans.

SUPPLY LIST

- ☐ At least one canned food item for each student
- ☐ Permanent markers
- ☐ Bibles
- ☐ Bible concordance
- ☐ Scratch paper
- ☐ Pens or pencils
- ☐ Rags or paper towels

do ahead Ask each student to bring in one or more canned food item. Have some extras on hand for those who visit or forget to bring one.

INSTRUCTIONS

1. Wipe or wash the bottoms of the cans.

2. Practice writing on a piece of scratch paper a phrase or verse that tells of God's forgiveness.

3. Write the phrase of encouragement on the bottom of the can.

4. Pray for the recipients of the cans, that they might know in a new way that God is loving and forgiving.

5. Deliver the cans to a food pantry for distribution to the needy.

SAMPLE MESSAGES AND SCRIPTURE REFERENCES

- No sin is too great for God to forgive.
- Jesus will forgive you. You only have to ask.
- Jesus wants to forgive you.
- Jesus died for your sins.
- 1 John 1:9
- Matthew 20:28
- Galatians 3:13a
- 1 Timothy 2:6

PROJECT WRAP-UP!

Jesus took the punishment for our sin—death and separation from God on the cross—so that we can be forgiven and have a relationship with God. Jesus has the authority to forgive sin. All we have to do is ask for forgiveness, and He will cleanse us of our sin.

- **What does it mean to you that Jesus forgives your sins?** *(that I can talk to God with confidence, that I don't have to be afraid, that there is no sin too great to keep me from God, etc.)*

- **What does the memory verse teach about forgiveness?** *(that God is ready and willing to forgive all my sins, that God is faithful to do what He promises, that I can't earn His forgiveness through my works, etc.)*

- **Do you have trouble accepting that Jesus forgives you? Explain.**

- **Do you ever feel like you have to do something to earn forgiveness? Explain.**

- **Since Jesus will forgive you without you needing to "work it off" or earn the forgiveness, what does that teach about forgiving others?** *(I should forgive someone without making them "work it off" in some way, I can show others how Jesus forgives by practicing it myself, etc.)*

- **Why should you try to not sin, even though Jesus offers forgiveness so freely?** *(because I want to show Him I love Him, because it cost Jesus a lot to take my sins upon Himself, because God calls us to live in a way that honors Him, etc.)*

Hang On

Plant wildflower seeds.

BIBLE BASIS:
Mark 10:17–21

MEMORY VERSE:
*For the word of God
is living and active.
Sharper than any
double-edged sword,
it penetrates even to
dividing soul and spirit,
joints and marrow; it
judges the thoughts and
attitudes of the heart.*
Hebrews 4:12

BIBLE BACKGROUND

You will never see Charlie Brown's good buddy, Linus, without his security blanket. It's what gets him through each day. Believe it or not, we are all just like Linus. Though that might seem a stretch to you at first, Linus shows us something about people—about ourselves. None of us likes to feel insecure. And we work awfully hard to avoid situations or circumstances that make us feel that way.

The rich young man who asked Jesus what he had to do to inherit eternal life had his own kind of security blanket. His was his great wealth. Though he had lived his whole life according to Jewish law, and he even recognized who Jesus was, when Jesus told him to give up his "security blanket," he couldn't do it. He wouldn't do it. He clung too tightly to his possessions. He wouldn't let go of them and accept the life Jesus offered.

Think about what makes you feel insecure. Then think about what you grasp hold of for security to help you feel better when life seems shaky or when things get out of control. If Jesus asked you to give it up, could you? Would you be willing to?

Jesus wants us to depend on Him, and Him alone. That doesn't mean we won't ever need or possess material things or anything else that might give us security. But it does mean that we don't hold onto anything so tightly that we depend on it for security rather than Jesus.

PROJECT

Students will plant wildflower seeds.

GOALS

- To challenge students to consider what they depend on for security
- To help students understand that Jesus cares for them more than they can imagine
- To beautify an area with wildflowers

TEACHER'S TIPS

Wildflower seeds can be sown with little soil preparation. Choose seeds that grow well in your area. If you have frequent rain, the seeds should do especially well without tending.

Choose a site that is wild, rough, and not landscaped. An open field, a wild area around the parking lot, or any other area left natural are possible places to plant your seeds. They will need good sun exposure to grow and bloom. If the site is on private property, be sure to obtain permission ahead of time.

If yours is an arid climate with little rain, your seeds may take regular watering to get established. If that is the case, and no irrigation or watering will be possible, consider planting the seeds in pots to establish them, then transplanting them later, or let the students take them home and enjoy watching them grow under their own care. Rakes, buckets, and peat moss will not be necessary if planting in pots.

SUPPLY LIST

- ☐ Wildflower seeds, in packets or divided into plastic baggies
- ☐ Watering cans with sprinkle heads
- ☐ Water
- ☐ Rakes (hand rakes or full size)
- ☐ Buckets
- ☐ Peat moss

do ahead Scout out a good area to plant wildflower seeds within walking distance of your church.

INSTRUCTIONS

1. Read Luke 12:22-31 to the students.

2. Distribute seeds so each student has some to sow.

3. Fill the watering cans with water.

4. Divide the peat moss into buckets for easier carrying.

5. Divide up the watering cans, rakes, and peat moss buckets to students willing to carry them to your destination.

6. Take a "walking field trip" to the pre-determined planting site.

7. Lightly rake, if possible, the area where seeds will be scattered.

8. Sow the seeds into the soil.

9. Cover the area with a thin layer of peat moss, and rake lightly again.

10. Sprinkle with water.

PROJECT WRAP-UP!

The Bible tells us that if God provides so beautifully for the flowers of the field, then we can be certain He will provide even more for us, who are uniquely precious to Him. We need not look for security in other places, for God has what we need.

- **Why do you think people worry about things they can't control?** *(it seems like it might help change the situation, they don't trust God to work in the situation, they're used to others worrying so they think it's normal, they've just never thought about what they're doing, etc.)*

- **What makes you feel insecure?** *(when my parents fight, when I'm around other kids who are popular and have lots of friends, when I'm expected to do something I'm not good at, etc.)*

- **What do you cling to to help you deal with your insecurities?** *(my friends, succeeding in my hobby, my outward appearance, choices about food, etc.)*

- **If Jesus asked you to give up what you cling to, would you be willing to? How would you do that?** *(stop using food—too much or too little—to make myself feel better, stop hanging out with certain kids that aren't good for me, stop worrying so much about how I look and what I wear, etc.)*

- **Share about a time you depended on God for help instead of something that usually gives you security.** *(Answers may vary.)*

Possibly the Impossible

Make candy bundles with notes of hope.

BIBLE BASIS:
Luke 1:26–38

MEMORY VERSE:
"What is impossible with men is possible with God."
Luke 18:27

BIBLE BACKGROUND

Imagine being a teenager, sitting in your room, doing your homework, and a blinding light flashes by your fish tank. You swivel in your desk chair, and there stands the biggest angel you've ever seen. (Okay, so it's the *only* angel you've ever seen.) That would be spectacular, not to mention frightening, unbelievable, shocking, disruptive, and countless other things. It would be hard to process what the angel says to you, let alone accept and submit to it.

But that's a lot like what happened to Mary. She was going about her business, and suddenly, there was Gabriel. He brought a message to her that wouldn't have been easy to hear. What he told her would disrupt her life, probably destroy her reputation (a *very* important thing in her time, in any time), drive away her fiancé, and ruin her chance at a normal life with a respectable husband. And it would produce a baby when it was impossible by human standards and leave her with a child to raise.

But Mary knew God. She knew He could do impossible things. She asked Gabriel how she could have a child when she knew she couldn't be pregnant. The angel answered that by God's power she would give birth, and her son would be called the Son of God. She accepted what the angel told her and believed God's way was best, even if it sounded amazing and improbable. She believed that what was impossible for man was possible for God.

Even if you never encounter an angel, sometimes the promises in God's Word can seem pretty unbelievable and amazing. But it's when we learn to trust God enough to take Him at His Word and step out in faith to obey that word, that the impossible will be done.

PROJECT

Students will make small packages of candies, bundled in tulle netting and tied with ribbons, with messages of hope attached. The bundles will be delivered to a local shelter or rescue mission.

GOALS

- To allow students to learn that though it may seem impossible to impact the lives of others so distant, God can take their efforts and use them for His purposes
- To bless others with a small gift to remind them they are cared for

TEACHER'S TIPS

Some students will be able to create their own messages without difficulty, while others may struggle for an idea. If you feel your class will do well creating their messages, have a sample or two available for suggestions. If you have students who may have difficulty, write or print up messages ahead of time, then have the students sign their names and add personal touches to the note.

Some examples for the notes are:

- As you enjoy this candy, know that you are remembered and cared for.
- I made this candy bundle especially for you to let you know I care.
- Our class made this especially for you. Have a blessed day!
- We pray you'll see God's love in a special way today.

Arrange to deliver your bundles to a shelter—perhaps the shelter where you've established a relationship on a previous project. Encourage students to accompany you to personally give and distribute the bundles.

SUPPLY LIST

- ☐ Wrapped candies, such as chocolates or small candy bars
- ☐ Red and/or green tulle (1 yard of 54" tulle makes fifteen 10"squares)
- ☐ Decorative ribbon (18" per bundle)
- ☐ Paper strips (5/8" x 8 ½")
- ☐ Pens
- ☐ Scissors
- ☐ Bibles

INSTRUCTIONS

1. Cut the tulle into 10" x 10" squares.

2. Write an encouraging note on the paper strip. Decorate as desired.

3. Place the paper strip on a tulle square, one end in the center and the other end over an edge of the tulle.

4. Fill the center of the tulle netting with candies, laying them on top of the paper strip.

5. Pull the edges of the tulle up together, creating a bundle around the candies. Have the paper strip stick out of the top.

6. Tie a ribbon around the "neck" of the bundle. (Use a partner to help.)

7. Plan a time to deliver the bundles together.

PROJECT WRAP-UP!

Sometimes we feel insignificant for various reasons, and we believe we're unable to make a difference in the world. But with God, nothing is impossible. He can take our humble actions and make them meaningful for His kingdom.

- **What do you think a miracle is?** *(Answers may vary, so allow for thoughtful discussion.)*

- **What are some miracles described in the Bible?** *(when Jesus raised Lazarus from the dead, turning water into wine, the Israelites leaving Egypt, etc.)*

- **What are some miracles, or impossible things done by God, that you know of today?** *(Answers will vary, and may include news stories or personal stories.)*

- **What has God done in your life that you couldn't have done yourself or that you thought was impossible?** *(He gave me a friend when I needed one, He healed my grandmother when the doctors said she wouldn't get better, etc.)*

- **Share about a time when you or someone you know made an important difference for a stranger?** *(my dad helped a lady change her tire, I shared my lunch with a boy who forgot his, etc.)*

- **Do you think something has to be huge and spectacular to be a miracle, or can it be small yet meaningful to one person? Explain.**

- **How do you think giving a message of hope to a stranger can be used by God?** *(it can encourage someone, it can show someone she isn't alone, it can help someone know of God's love in a new way, etc.)*

Shout It Out

Go Christmas caroling to spread the Good News.

BIBLE BASIS:
Luke 2:1–20

MEMORY VERSE:
Today in the town of David a Savior has been born to you; he is Christ the Lord.
Luke 2:11

BIBLE BACKGROUND

Think of a time when you received really good news or something amazing happened to you. How did you respond? You likely didn't keep it to yourself. It's probably a good guess that you told whomever you could; that you shared the news and wanted others to know. You might have even jumped three feet off the ground, whooped louder than a yodeling cowboy, and made a scene that would have been slightly embarrassing if anyone had seen you.

The shepherds we read about in Luke were working the night shift, keeping track of their flocks of sheep, going about their usual shepherd duties. Then all at once, just like with Mary when Gabriel appeared, an angel made a surprise visit.

The glory of the Lord—probably something that looked like light and energy—shined on them, and the shepherds were scared out of their sandals. The angel calmed them down, told them of Jesus' birth, and where they would find Him.

Then the whole sky filled with angels. They were everywhere, praising and worshiping God. Close your eyes and imagine for a moment what that would look and sound like!

After the angels left, the shepherds went into Bethlehem and found Jesus, just as the angel had said. They started telling everyone about the Holy Child they had found. The news was so good, the shepherds couldn't keep it to themselves. It was so amazing, even angels had to talk about it!

PROJECT

Students will proclaim the good news of Jesus' birth by singing. They will use Christmas carols with messages of Christ's birth, love, and hope to tell others the great message of Christmas.

GOALS

- To proclaim the good news of Jesus' birth
- To help students understand the importance of spreading the word about Jesus
- To bless others with Christmas caroling

TEACHER'S TIPS

Pre-arrange with a nursing home, senior citizen facility, or hospital (such as a pediatric wing or waiting area) to visit and sing. Contact the activities director, and determine the best area or wing to visit.

Ask the activities director for any restrictions or instructions necessary to comply with facility needs or regulations.

If planning the caroling during regular meeting hours, arrange chaperones and transportation ahead of time to be available. If your caroling will take place at another time, determine a meeting time and place. If you choose to sing outdoors, make sure your students know to wear weather-appropriate clothing.

A fun culmination to caroling is to enjoy hot cocoa and cookies. You can provide this yourself or ask parents to bring thermoses of hot chocolate and plates of goodies. Arrange with the activity director as necessary for a place to enjoy your treats.

SUPPLY LIST

- ☐ Consent forms from parents if leaving the usual meeting place
- ☐ Caroling books or song sheets, with words or music
- ☐ Pre-arranged location to visit
- ☐ Drivers or transportation to take your group to the facility
- ☐ Hot chocolate and cookies

do ahead Send home permission slips and information as necessary for parental consent if leaving your normal meeting site or if you will be caroling at a time other than your normal meeting time.

INSTRUCTIONS

In-class preparation:

1. Have students select carols to sing and the order to sing them. (You may want to have several options available ahead of time.)

2. Practice the chosen carols.

3. Discuss expected behavior appropriate for your selected location.

Day of activity:

1. Arrive and gather at the facility.

2. Sing carols proclaiming the good news of Christmas.

3. Remember to smile for your audience!

4. Keep talking and horseplay contained.

5. Have fun.

6. Enjoy the treats when you've finished singing.

PROJECT WRAP-UP!

When Jesus was born, even the angels couldn't help but show up in the heavens and spread the word. They filled the skies with praise and worship, telling of the good news.

- **What do you do when you have good news?** (*tell everyone I see, wait to tell so I can enjoy having a special secret, scream and shout, etc.*)

- **How do you feel about telling others about Jesus?** (*it makes me nervous, I love to talk about Jesus, I can't do it but wish I could, etc.*)

- **Share about a time when you told someone about Jesus.**

- **How have others shared the news of Jesus with you?** (*in Sunday school, when I have discussions with my friends, my parents talk to me about Him, etc.*)

- **How do you feel when you are told about Jesus?** (*it makes me happy, I get uncomfortable, I worry about what others think, etc.*)

- **Who would you like to tell about Jesus, and when could you do so in a natural, comfortable way?** (*Answers may vary.*)

Got Any Change?

Host a game and snack get-together and invite new kids for a change.

BIBLE BASIS:
Luke 3:7–14

MEMORY VERSE:
Whoever claims to live in him must walk as Jesus did. 1 John 2:6

BIBLE BACKGROUND

Consider the character Edmund in the movie *Narnia*. At the beginning of the story, he is selfish and destructive. But he eventually realizes the error of his ways and essentially repents (though he doesn't avoid some consequences). Once he repents, he develops into an entirely different person, becoming caring, selfless, and humble. He even sacrifices his life in the fight against the white witch to save his siblings.

Edmund's story is a great example of repentance. He changes his actions and alters his path. He becomes more like the model of love and self-sacrifice that Aslan portrays.

True repentance brings changes in our behavior. There should be good "fruit" apparent from our actions. In Luke 3:7-14, John the Baptist teaches how that should look. We should share what we have with those less fortunate. We should have a shift in attitude that takes us from greed to gratitude and from self-centeredness to generosity.

Repentance with no change is empty. It would be like hitting a friend, telling that friend you are sorry for hitting him, but continuing to pummel him as you say it. You must redirect your action, just as Edmund did.

Then, as we change our path, we begin to develop into a new person, into the person God intended for us to be. It is then that we walk as Jesus did.

PROJECT

Students will plan and host a game and snack get-together, with intentional efforts to invite and include kids from school and other groups or organizations that are notably on the fringes or in no identifiable group or clique.

GOALS

- To enable students to change their usual behavior by interacting with others they would not normally spend time and/or energy on
- To bless others who may feel unwanted or on the fringe
- To build new relationships
- To have fun and fellowship

TEACHER'S TIPS

It can be really tough to reach out to outsiders as an adolescent. But how helpful it would be to make them more aware of cliques and the harm of exclusion before destructive patterns of behavior are solidified.

Encourage your students to "get in the shoes" of kids who are outcasts. Help them find ways through discussion and reflection to recognize and overcome their fears about interacting with kids different than themselves.

Ask them what it is that keeps them from reaching out to others. Ask them to explore their fears, their insecurities, and their beliefs about those who are different. Help them find new perspectives and specific actions they can take to change their established patterns of behavior.

To prepare, ask these same questions of yourself. It will enable you to better lead your group as they explore these issues with you.

SUPPLY LIST

- ☐ Board games
- ☐ Snacks
- ☐ Drinks
- ☐ Invitations
- ☐ School, group, and organization directories or phone books
- ☐ Location, date, and time
- ☐ Nametags

INSTRUCTIONS

During the planning stage:

1. Determine what board or parlor games will be played at the events. Set up stations, rotating every fifteen minutes at the sound of a bell, whether or not the game is finished. Choose interactive and high-energy games, as well as those that have short, fast rounds and turn over quickly. Games that are familiar or easy to learn will work best.

2. Plan the snacks. Bring snacks to share, or if the budget allows, have the class provide the chips, cookies, and drinks.

3. Plan an icebreaker. Incorporate an activity early on that includes names, so everyone has a chance to learn names and something about each other. Plan to use nametags as well.

4. Create your guest list. Include kids outside of your normal circles of friends. Make the invitations, and decide how to deliver them.

5. As the date nears, be flexible and invite anyone you think might be interested, but use the written invitation to let those on your guest list know they are specifically welcomed.

On event day:

1. Wear a nametag. Meet and greet your guests as they arrive, and provide them with a nametag. Help them feel comfortable by inviting them to enjoy some snacks, including them in conversation, and introducing them to others.

2. Explain the rules of the event. Demonstrate the bell sound, so everyone will know when it's time to switch stations.

3. Play games. Have fun. Take note of names, and get to know new friends.

4. Have more snacks. Wrap up the event by thanking your guests for coming.

PROJECT WRAP-UP!

When God calls us to repentance, He expects that we will change our behavior. Changing usually takes an intentional decision. It doesn't just happen. Sometimes it's hard. Sometimes we fail and have to try again. And again. But He wants to help us, and He wants us to keep trying.

- **What behavior have you tried to change but haven't been able to?** *(fighting with my sibling, disobeying my parents, thinking about something I know isn't pleasing to God, lack of friendliness, etc.)*

- **Give an example of a time you've successfully changed an action or behavior for the better.** *(Answers will vary.)*

- **What did it take to accomplish that successful change?** *(God helped me have the strength, I got help from others who knew I was trying to change, etc.)*

- **What is something you'd like to change now?** *(Answers will vary.)*

- **What can you do in the upcoming days and weeks to help make that change?** *(pray, talk to a friend/teacher/parent, avoid a situation that allows me to easily continue in the pattern I want to change, etc.)*

Mission Possible

Visit a thrift store and create an outfit.

BIBLE BASIS:
Luke 4:16–22

MEMORY VERSE:
But seek first his kingdom and his righteousness, and all these things will be given to you as well.
Matthew 6:33

BIBLE BACKGROUND

Imagine getting on your bike. Now imagine that you're told, "Race like the wind! You don't have a lot of time. They're waiting for you." You pedal like you've had way too many energy drinks, and off you go.

But wait a minute. Where are you going? How can you go when you don't even know where you're going? You can't. You have to know your destination before you take off in order to even start in the right direction, let alone continue correctly toward your goal.

Jesus knew where He was going. He knew His mission, why He had come to earth, and what His life was all about.

Think for a moment about who you are. In one or two sentences, how would you define yourself, your purpose, your "destiny"? It's important to know that about yourself if you are to follow the right path. You can't very well get where you're going if you don't know where it is you're headed.

Our calling is similar, in many ways, to Jesus' calling. As part of His calling, He came to help the poor, the oppressed, the captive, and the disabled. Those are the same things we are to do. Because we follow Christ, our task is to continue His mission, to follow the example He set. The only way we can carry out this duty, however, is by staying on the path of God's Word. Scripture will lead us on the road to fulfill our destiny.

PROJECT

The class will divide into teams, shop with their team at a thrift store, choose an entire outfit for someone the size/age of their choosing, and deliver it to a shelter or needy person.

GOALS

- To enable students to care for the poor in a tangible way
- To allow students an opportunity to use their own resources to make a difference for someone else
- To let students use their creativity and sense of fashion for the benefit of others

TEACHER'S TIPS

Encourage the students to take seriously what they are doing and to put together an outfit they themselves would like. It might be easy to be silly and find clothes that are unusual or goofy. Remind them that the goal is to truly bless someone who might otherwise be unable to acquire nice or stylish clothes.

Suggest to them different scenarios, so they might catch a vision for the person who will benefit from their efforts. Such scenarios might include a woman needing a fashionable outfit for job interviews so she can better provide for her children. Another could be a student their own age who doesn't have money to purchase updated clothes, but would enjoy being able to dress more like their friends at school.

The more of a realistic "face" you can attach to the individual for whom they are shopping, the easier it will be for them to take a personal interest in the project and have it hold more meaning for them.

When you arrange with the shelter or mission to donate the clothes, make it known that the items will be purchased with the intent of furnishing complete outfits, and confirm that they will be passed on in their intended sets. Also, communicate to the receiving shelter that any feedback they could give to the class regarding the disbursement and receipt of the clothes would be helpful to hear.

Consider holding a fundraiser such as a bake sale or car wash, or encourage the students to earn the money, instead of simply having children bring money in.

SUPPLY LIST

- ☐ Shelter or mission (perhaps one with which your class has previously established a relationship)
- ☐ $3 - $5 from each student
- ☐ Identify thrift store
- ☐ Note card
- ☐ Self-addressed stamped envelope, one for each group
- ☐ Pens

Greetings!

As a group project for our Sunday school class, we worked together to coordinate and provide an outfit for you. We hope you like it! Though we don't know you, we've said a prayer for you. We hope you experience God's love in some new way today.

We've included an envelope for your use if you'd like to let us know anything about yourself. We'd love to hear anything you want to share about how you were able to use or enjoy the clothes.

Blessings,

(Your class name)

INSTRUCTIONS

1. Break into groups.

2. Each group should determine for whom they will be shopping: age/ size/gender.

3. Decide what kind of outfit you are looking for: dressy/casual/sporty.

4. Write a note, together as a group, to the intended recipient, with a message of care and intent. Include a self-addressed, stamped envelope (using the church's address and class name to protect the privacy of individuals). (See sample note for ideas.)

5. Determine how much money each person will contribute.

6. Plan a time to meet and shop.

7. Arrange rides within the group (check with parents and ask for their assistance), and meet at a designated time and place.

8. Have fun shopping!

9. When the outfits are purchased, have groups meet with the rest of the class to show each other what items they've purchased for the outfits.

10. Pray together for the recipients that the clothes will be a blessing to them, and that they will better understand God's love for them.

11. Have someone from each group carefully wash and prepare the items to give to the shelter. Explain your expectations for how the clothes should look when returned to you (ironed and folded?). The outfits should be brought back to you for delivery.

12. Deliver outfits to the shelter.

PROJECT WRAP-UP!

Jesus came to take care of the poor and humble. He wants us to do the same.

- **How do you normally perceive the poor?** *(I don't really think about them much, they make me sad, I don't understand why they are poor, etc.)*

- **How has this project changed the way you think of people less fortunate than yourself?** *(Answers will vary.)*

- **What was most fun for you in this project?** *(knowing what we did could really help someone, being creative with colors and styles, etc.)*

- **What was most difficult?** *(finding the interest to care about someone I don't even know, using my own money for a stranger, not being able to buy brand-new things for someone, etc.)*

- **What can you do in the future to be more caring and loving toward those who are in need?** *(continue to pray for the person I shopped for, do other projects for the needy, put myself in their place to think about how I could be a blessing, etc.)*

- **What new thing did you learn about yourself through this project?** *(I'm not as generous as I would like to be, I really have a love for the poor, helping others really makes me happy, etc.)*

Let 'Em Have It!

Create children's activity packets for Laundromats.

BIBLE BASIS:
Luke 9:51–56;
Matthew 5:38–48

MEMORY VERSE:
But, I tell you: Love your enemies and pray for those who persecute you.
Matthew 5:44

BIBLE BACKGROUND

As Jesus was traveling to Jerusalem, He went through Samaria. But the people living in a certain Samaritan village did not welcome Him. That made Jesus' disciples very angry, and they wanted to call fire down on them from heaven to destroy them.

But Jesus wouldn't let them do that. He even rebuked them for suggesting such a thing.

When someone hurts or upsets you, do you ever want to get revenge against them? At times, in our darker moments, we may even wish we could supernaturally call down fire from the sky onto their heads. (Thankfully, we can't, and our better judgments, prompted by God's righteous conviction, generally prevail.)

Think of your favorite adventure movie. Probably someone who represents good battles against evil throughout most of the story. Then in the end, when the bad guys are defeated, it feels so satisfying to see the good guy let 'em have it!

But as Christians, we aren't supposed to carry out vengeance against others. When we let 'em have it, the "it" we should let them have is love. We are to show mercy and at the same time trust God to give mercy or justice, according to His purpose. God calls us to respond with kindness. This can include people we don't know as well as "enemies." Being kind to someone you don't even know is a wonderful way to demonstrate God's love.

PROJECT

Students will assemble activity packets for children and place them in a coin-operated laundry facility for patrons of the business to use.

GOALS

- To perform a loving act for others you do not know
- To bless others by providing not only fun activities for children, but to help parents occupy their children as they wash their laundry

TEACHER'S TIPS

Contact local coin-operated laundry facilities and obtain permission as needed to place activity packets in their facilities.

When you send home information about the project, include a description of the project and why you are doing it.

Consider asking students to sign up for specific items to avoid everyone bringing in a box of crayons and no one bringing zipper bags. Ask them for any additional ideas of items they would like to include that aren't on the list.

The crayons can be divided as needed and a few colors put in each packet. Pages can be removed from the color or activity books and a few put in each packet. To remove pages easily, fold the page as close to the binding as possible. Then carefully and slowly tear the page from the book.

SUPPLY LIST

- ☐ Gallon-sized, plastic zipper bags
- ☐ Crayons
- ☐ Coloring books or pages
- ☐ Activity pages, such as dot-to-dot or maze puzzles
- ☐ Stickers
- ☐ Bubble and wand bottles
- ☐ Play dough
- ☐ Jacks and bouncy ball
- ☐ Plain paper for notes
- ☐ Markers for writing messages

Send home information at least a week in advance to inform students and their parents of the upcoming project. Ask them to bring the supplies listed, as able, to include in the activity packets.

Have one or more of your messages of greeting translated into Spanish or another language common in your region.

INSTRUCTIONS

1. Split your class into groups.

2. Divide the supplies into equal amounts and give some to each group. Each group may have more than one packet's worth of supplies if there are enough.

3. Place all supplies in a plastic zipper bag.

4. Write a note of cheer on a sheet of paper that will show well through one side of the plastic bag.

5. Zip the bag closed.

6. Pray for the recipients of the packets.

7. Deliver to a local coin-operated laundry facility (or to more than one if you have enough packets).

Sample messages to insert into packets:

■ Greetings, Friend! We made this activity packet for your children to help them have fun while you work. We hope they enjoy what's inside!

■ We know it's hard for kids to be patient while waiting on laundry. We hope this makes your time here a little easier.

■ Hi! Please enjoy this packet, our gift to you and your children. We hope it brightens your day today!

PROJECT WRAP-UP!

God calls us to respond to others with love. Even if they don't seem to deserve it, we are to be kind and even give more to them than they are seeking.

- **When do you find it especially hard to respond with love?** *(when my brother won't stop bugging me, when what happens to me is unfair, when someone is getting away with something, etc.)*

- **Describe a time when you wanted to "get back" at someone. What did you decide to do?** *(Answers may vary.)*

- **Have you ever done something nice for someone you didn't know? What happened?** *(Answers may vary.)*

- **Has someone ever done something nice for you, even though they had never met you? If so, how did that make you feel?** *(I was surprised, I wondered why they did it, it made me feel good, etc.)*

- **What are some ways to show kindness to someone you don't know?** *(Answers may vary.)*

- **If someone makes you mad, what can you do to show kindness and to respond with love?** *(walk away, forgive them, etc.)*

- **When has God responded to you with love, even though you didn't deserve it?** *(when He died on the cross, when He takes care of me, when He forgives my sins, etc.)*

Thank God!

Send letters of thanks and care packages to soldiers.

BIBLE BASIS:
Luke 17:11–19

MEMORY VERSE:
"We give thanks to you, Lord God Almighty, the One who is and who was, because you have taken your great power and have begun to reign." Revelation 11:17

BIBLE BACKGROUND

Samaria was a land where the Israelites had been exiled many, many years before Jesus' time, when they were conquered and taken from their land. During the hundreds of years they lived in Samaria, the Israelites inter-married and took on the lifestyle and beliefs of the local people, becoming unfaithful to the true God, the God of Israel. It was because of this unfaithfulness that the Jews of Galilee despised the Samaritans.

Jesus was traveling along the border of Samaria and Galilee when He met 10 men infected with leprosy, a disease that made its victims "unclean" and unable to live among other members of the community. The 10 men recognized Jesus and called out to Him from a distance for mercy. Jesus told them to go to the priests, the officials who could pro-nounce them "clean" and allow them to rejoin their community.

As the 10 men went, they were all healed. One of the men, a Samaritan, came running back. He threw himself down at Jesus' feet, praising God in a loud voice. Though Jews despised his people, the Samaritan risked approaching Jesus, touching and speaking to Him. Jesus asked, "Where are the other nine?"

They had failed to give Jesus thanks. The Samaritan was the only one to acknowledge what God had done and to proclaim his gratitude for the gift of healing.

And Jesus took notice.

How do you respond when God blesses you? Will Jesus be asking where you are when He's given you a blessing? Or will you be like the Samaritan, who risked much yet still returned to praise and thank God?

PROJECT

Students will prepare a letter of thanks along with care packages to send to those serving in the military.

GOALS

- To allow students to thank God for what He has done for them
- To encourage students to consider what others have done that is worthy of gratitude and then to express that gratitude

TEACHER'S TIPS

Help your students understand the sacrifices the members of the armed services make. Help them know our freedom over the decades and centuries has been protected and secured by soldiers, and they deserve our gratitude for all they do.

If you don't have a local agency or connection for sending troops care packages and letters, they can be found through the Internet. To prepare for this project, determine which agency you will work through to send your letters and packages.

Some organizations accept donations and provide the care package, based on requirements for safety and security. Some give guidelines for the type of items to be sent, such as sunscreen, socks, toiletries, snacks, and phone cards, as well as how to package and mail them. Check with the U.S. Postal Service about free boxes to use for shipping.

SUPPLY LIST

- ☐ List of names of service personnel to whom you will be sending letters/packages
- ☐ Note cards or stationery, and envelopes
- ☐ Boxes for care packages
- ☐ Bubble wrap, or other light-weight packing material
- ☐ Items to send (based on agency suggestions and restrictions)
- ☐ Packing tape
- ☐ Mailing labels
- ☐ Waterproof marker

do ahead Consider using funds raised through your "Man Does Not Live by Cupcakes Alone" bake sale. Or, if you don't have a budget to pay postage or purchase items, ask the students ahead of time to arrive with an offering or set dollar amount to cover the expenses. Or let your entire church take part in your project by collecting a special offering from your congregation.

INSTRUCTIONS

Before meeting to assemble packages and write letters:

1. Contact the agency with whom you will be working to obtain names of service personnel and instructions for preparing and mailing letters and/or packages.

2. Determine the source for items in packages. If students will be bringing donations to send, instruct them ahead of time what to bring to class.

During class time:

1. Break into groups.

2. Give each group a box to fill.

3. Divide items equally among groups.

4. Assign each soldier's name to a student(s).

5. Write letters of appreciation.

6. Prepare letters and boxes for mailing according to the instructions from the agency with which you are working.

PROJECT WRAP-UP!

There is much to be grateful for, and it is important to take time to consider what God has done. It also is important to show gratitude to others. Doing so will help you develop a sense of thankfulness and help you avoid taking things for granted or assuming you are entitled to receive blessings.

- **What has God done for you that you are thankful for?** *(He sent Jesus to die for me, He has provided a home/family/friends, He comforts me when I've had trouble, etc.)*

- **How often do you take time to thank God for His goodness?** *(every day, when something good happens, I don't think about it much, etc.)*

- **When do you find it hard to thank God?** *(when I'm down, when bad things happen, when things are going good and I forget about God, etc.)*

- **What can you thank God for even if circumstances are hard or when bad things happen?** *(that He loves me and never leaves me, that He can make even the bad things turn out for my benefit, etc.)*

- **What has someone done for you that you would like to show gratitude for?** *(the sacrifices my parents have made so I can ___, a friend supported me during a tough time, etc.)*

- **Why do you think it is important to show gratitude to others?** *(then I won't forget that God takes care of me, to encourage others who help, to let others know their help is important, etc.)*

- **What can you do in the upcoming week to show gratitude to God or others for their gifts?** *(write a thank-you note, tell my parents I appreciate what they have done, spend time each day praying and thanking God for His blessings, etc.)*

Dear Sgt. Johnson,

I'm writing to you to say 'Thank You' for all you do as you serve our country. It can't be easy to be away from your loved ones. I bet it is hard to live in a place where conditions are tough, and to be in danger, too.

I'd like to tell you a little about myself. I'm in seventh grade, and my Sunday school class is learning about being thankful, both to God and to others. I really like to

(over)

Hearts Trump Diamonds

Make sweet treats to thank volunteers and caregivers for their service.

BIBLE BASIS:
Luke 18:9–14

MEMORY VERSE:
Man looks at the outward appearance, but the LORD looks at the heart.
1 Samuel 16:7

BIBLE BACKGROUND

Have you ever taken a bite of a scrumptious-looking piece of fruit and found that it was actually spoiled on the inside? A bit disappointing. Shocking even. Did you spit it out faster than you could say *pomegranate?* And what about a CZ—cubic zirconia? It may look like a fine diamond. They even make great stud earrings. But if you were to sell them, they wouldn't have a very high value.

Jesus told a parable that taught a lesson about people who look one way on the outside, but what's going on the inside—in their hearts—is a completely different story.

Pharisees in Jesus' time were considered by many to be authorities and experts on being righteous. And tax collectors were despised by many and considered cheats and scoundrels.

The Pharisee in Jesus' parable boasted to God about how wonderful he was and thanked God he was not wicked like others, including the tax collector.

The tax collector, on the other hand, was so humble and aware of his state of sin that he wouldn't go near the temple. But from a distance he beat himself and wouldn't raise his head toward God. He agonized over his sin and begged God for mercy.

It was the heart of the tax collector who gained God's mercy and not that of the Pharisee. Like the bad fruit, though the Pharisee appeared to be upright and good—and probably dressed better than anyone in his designer robes—his heart was rotten and foul. The tax collector, though he appeared too corrupt for redemption, humbled his heart before God and gained mercy.

PROJECT

Students will make treats for volunteers, teachers, pastors, and/or church staff to show appreciation for their service.

GOALS

- To allow students the opportunity to thank those who show their servant hearts by caring for others
- To bless those who serve in your church
- To help students look past any outward appearances—good or bad—and recognize people's hearts

TEACHER'S TIPS

Every church has people who work with a humble heart, quietly toiling behind the scenes and often gaining little recognition. Explore with your students which people of your congregation are like that, and make them the recipients of your efforts.

Use no-bake recipes, or ideas for treats like the ones that follow, if you wish to make them in class together without kitchen equipment. Or, if you wish to make more of a variety of baked goods, plan a time and place to meet outside of class to bake together and prepare your treats. Or, ask students to bring pre-made treats to share among recipients.

SUPPLY LIST

- ☐ Sturdy paper or plastic plates
- ☐ Plastic wrap
- ☐ Ingredients from recipe
- ☐ Mixing bowl
- ☐ Large spoons for mixing
- ☐ Note cards
- ☐ Markers

Gather recipe ingredients prior to class. Or, call students and ask that they bring an ingredient for the treats.

INSTRUCTIONS

1. Determine who will receive your thank-you treats.

2. Prepare the treats.

3. Divide and arrange the treats on plates.

4. Cover with plastic wrap.

5. Write thank-you notes, and include them on the plates.

6. Deliver to recipients.

In-class treat ideas:

■ Spread pre-made icing between graham crackers or butter cookies.

■ Mix together 2 cups of peanut butter and 3-4 cups of powdered sugar until stiff. Add a bag of chocolate chips. Roll into balls.

■ Mix an 8-ounce block of soft cream cheese with ½ cup honey. Serve with apples and an inexpensive apple slicer/corer.

■ Combine 8 ounces of soft cream cheese, ½ cup sugar, and ½ teaspoon vanilla. Spread between vanilla wafers (or use cream cheese icing in a tub).

■ Spread icing on pre-made sugar cookies and sprinkle with decorative toppings.

PROJECT WRAP-UP!

Jesus is concerned with your heart and your humility. New designer jeans, cool diamond earrings, or great hair days don't impress Him. Recognizing the need for His forgiveness is what will bring His mercy, not being grateful for being better than the kid at school who you think really blew it.

- **Why do you think we measure people by their appearance?** *(our culture teaches that, it's harder to look past appearances, etc.)*

- **Describe a time when you thought one way about a stranger, but then got to know him or her and found out you were wrong.** *(Answers may vary.)*

- **Have you ever had an experience when someone assumed incorrectly that you were something that you're not? Explain.**

- **What actions and habits do you use to rate how good of a Christian you or others are?** *(church attendance, language, wearing the proper styles, people you hang out with, etc.)* **What does today's story tell us about this?** *(Allow students time to discuss.)*

- **How does Jesus rate how good of a Christian you are?** *(He doesn't rate us like we would. He knows what's in our hearts and if we are humble and repentant.)*

- **Why must we pray like the tax collector and not the Pharisee?** *(because none of us is "good enough," Jesus doesn't "rate" our habits, without humility we won't have mercy, etc.)*

i m praying 4 u

Create a prayer chain for use among classmates.

BIBLE BASIS:
John 17:1, 6–9, 13–15, 20–24

MEMORY VERSE:
I urge, then, first of all, that requests, prayers, intercession and thanksgiving be made for everyone.
1 Timothy 2:1

BIBLE BACKGROUND

Jesus knew He was about to be separated from His friends and companions. He wouldn't have them by His side for the upcoming torture, humiliation, and horrible death that He would face. Yet, He took time to pray, committing to God His disciples, their ministry that would continue after He left, and all those who would become believers because of the disciples' ministry.

Jesus communicates to His Father that His disciples "get it." They have heard God's message through Jesus and have accepted it. They believe and know that Jesus came from God. And Jesus lifts them up to God the Father for this.

Jesus asked God to protect them from the evil one. Jesus had given them protection and kept them safe while He was in the world with them. But as He anticipated His departure, He recognized the need for God's protection and asked that God provide for their safekeeping.

He also asked for their sanctification—the process by which God would transform them to be more Christ-like. Jesus asked that God the Father would sanctify them by His Word, which is truth.

Jesus commended—or entrusted the care of—His disciples to the Father. He showed us how we can pray for others. We can entrust others into God's care, just as Jesus did by lifting them up to the Father in prayer.

PROJECT

Students will develop a prayer chain for use among their classmates.

GOALS

- To teach students how to pray for one another
- To encourage students to commit to lifting each other up in prayer regularly
- To provide a way to learn of prayer needs and a system to carry out prayer support

TEACHER'S TIPS

Stress to students the importance of confidentiality when participating in a prayer chain. One way to maintain confidentiality is to make sure that all prayer requests remain inside the prayer chain, and they are not shared with anyone else. Also, encourage students to take the prayer requests seriously and to not attempt to add to them or change them in any way.

Ask students how they feel they could best utilize and support the prayer chain. Help them explore different scenarios and how they might respond to them, such as receiving information that needs an adult to intervene or not being able to contact the next person.

By developing the system in a careful way upfront, you'll enable the class to maintain their prayer chain for a longer, more effective time period without burnout or frustration.

SUPPLY LIST

- ☐ Blank prayer tree chart or blank paper (1 per student)
- ☐ Pens
- ☐ Hat/container
- ☐ Slips of paper
- ☐ Make a chart that can be filled in or use this example of a phone tree chart.

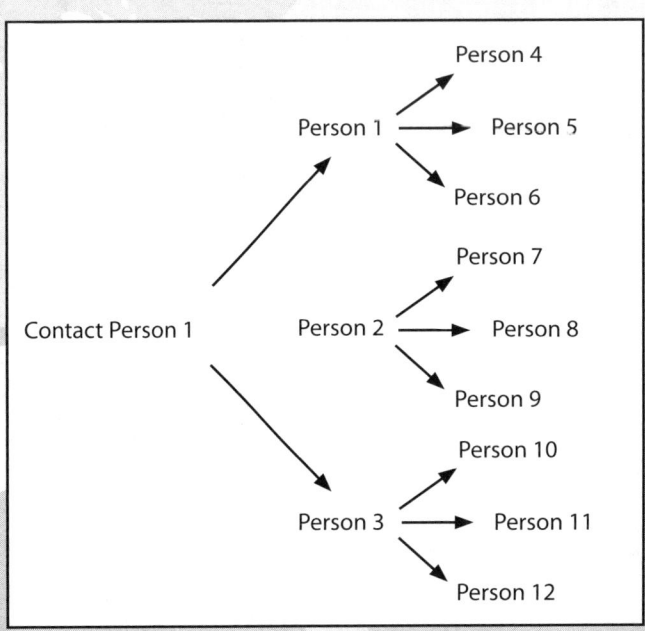

INSTRUCTIONS

1. Determine who the contact person will be to accept prayer requests and initiate the prayer phone tree.

2. Take volunteers for the first two to three contacts on the tree—depending on the size of your class—or place everyone's name in a hat and pull out two or three names.

3. For each name drawn/volunteered, determine two or three additional names, either through volunteers or by pulling names from the hat.

4. Continue assigning new people to each person on the tree. Write each name on the appropriate line of your prayer tree.

5. Collect contact information for each person. Determine if you will use e-mail groups, text messaging, or phone calls.

6. Set any parameters your group wishes to keep, such as type of requests, frequency, or eligibility (class members, family only, friends outside of class, etc.).

7. Discuss how best to use your prayer tree—emergency requests only, less-pressing needs on a daily basis, etc.

8. Make sure each person has a copy of the prayer tree to take home.

9. Determine what to do if your person to contact is unavailable.

10. Pray for the process of lifting up each other in prayer in the days to come.

PROJECT WRAP-UP!

Jesus prayed for His disciples and showed us how to pray for each other. It's important to support each other with prayer regularly.

- **Describe a time when someone prayed for you.** *(when I was sick, when my parents split up, when my grandpa passed away, etc.)*

- **How did knowing you were being prayed for help you?** *(it encouraged me and I didn't feel alone, it seemed like things got better, I knew I was cared for, etc.)*

- **In what tangible or real ways did you see that prayer made a difference?** *(the peace I felt was really different than usual, I felt stronger, etc.)*

- **When have you prayed for others in need?** *(a relative was really sick, my friend was depressed, etc.)*

- **What difference do you think it makes to pray for others?** *(God answers prayer, it lets people know they aren't forgotten, it can change the situation, it takes the focus off myself, etc.)*

- **What challenges do you think you'll face when you commit to being a part of a prayer chain?** *(remembering to pray, believing it makes a difference, etc.)*

Let's Do Lunch

Make lunches for the homeless.

BIBLE BASIS:
John 21:3–17

MEMORY VERSE:
"I have loved you with an everlasting love; I have drawn you with loving-kindness."
Jeremiah 31:3

BIBLE BACKGROUND

Think of a time you let someone down who is important to you. You probably felt really bad afterward. Maybe thoughts kept going through your head about it, like shame and disappointment in yourself. It's hard when we fail someone special to us.

Peter did that. He loved Jesus and only wanted to please Him. But when things got tough, he blew it. After Jesus had been taken prisoner, Peter skipped out on Him just like the other disciples did. He hid among the crowd, watching from a distance, but doing nothing to help Jesus. And when people recognized him and said he was with Jesus, he denied that he even knew Jesus. Three times he denied it.

But Jesus loved Peter so much He wanted to restore Peter. He wanted to help Peter get over the shame and guilt he felt for abandoning and denying Jesus.

After Jesus' resurrection, He met the disciples on the shore after they'd fished all night. He had prepared breakfast for them. But He was doing more than providing for their physical needs. He provided restoration to Peter. Three times Jesus asked Peter if he loved Him, giving Peter three chances to affirm their relationship. Then Jesus entrusted His followers to Peter's care. In spite of Peter's terrible failure, Jesus loved him and showed him immeasurable kindness.

We need to follow Jesus' example and do the same for others. We need to let people know that even though they may disappiont Him sometimes, God still loves them, and He is able to give them a brand-new start.

PROJECT

Students will prepare sack lunches to deliver to the homeless or needy in a shelter or a park.

GOALS

- To allow students to interact with the needy in society and provide them with a meal
- To bless someone in great need with a meal
- To encourage students to act out the love, compassion, and grace of Christ

TEACHER'S TIPS

It is often difficult to think of approaching and interacting with the homeless. Many are unwell emotionally and/or have unhealthy addictions. But Jesus demonstrated over and over again how much He loves and cares for the outcasts of society.

Prepare your students for this project ahead of time. Allow honest discussion. You may wish to use the questions from the Project Wrap-Up! both before and after the event, for preparation and debriefing.

Depending on the maturity of your students and whether or not they have ever interacted with the homeless before, you may opt to carry out this activity in a shelter instead of a park. A shelter with established rules and expectations would provide a more controlled environment. If you can find a shelter that provides overnight lodging but requires a prompt exit in the morning, you can hand out the lunches as the individuals leave the shelter. If you decide to visit the homeless in a park, be sure you have a strong adult-to-student ratio, and your students know to always stay with their group.

Whatever you decide, try to provide an experience for the students that will be a challenge and something different than what they may have already experienced. The purpose is to stretch them and help them consider new ways of thinking and acting. Interacting with the homeless can be a very unforgettable, rewarding experience.

SUPPLY LIST

- ☐ Paper lunch bags
- ☐ Plastic sandwich bags
- ☐ Bread
- ☐ Sandwich fixings (things that won't spoil)
- ☐ Chips
- ☐ Cookies or other treats
- ☐ Fruit
- ☐ Hard-boiled eggs
- ☐ Juice boxes
- ☐ Lip balm or small, travel-size hand lotion

 **to consider** Choose how your class will distribute the lunches. Arrange with agencies, if you are using them, the best time and method to give out lunches. If you plan to go to a public area to distribute to the homeless (something that might only be possible in larger, urban settings) check with rescue agencies or local authorities in the area to determine the best place or time. You may want to invite them to accompany your class on the project.

You'll need to round up supplies ahead of time. Send information home about the project. You might want to invite the parents to an informational meeting, at which time you can arrange chaperones and drivers.

INSTRUCTIONS

1. Prepare a clean area and wash hands.

2. Set up an assembly line to prepare lunches.

3. Make sandwiches.

4. Put chips or cookies into baggies, as needed.

5. Fill lunch bags with each of the food items, plus a lip balm or lotion.

6. Instruct students how to distribute the sacks when the time comes. Suggest saying, "We're from (your church name), and we'd like to give you a lunch we made for you. Would you like one?"

7. Go to the destination and hand out lunches.

A good time to deliver your lunches may be after your morning activities and worship are over. Set up drivers and chaperones to meet after church. If you are unable to deliver them the same day, consider meeting at another time to assemble the lunches and then take them to distribute.

PROJECT WRAP-UP!

God has grace for us when we disappoint Him. He knows when we struggle. When we turn back to him, we find He demonstrates love and compassion. God wants us to help others experience His loving grace, no matter what difficult situation they are facing.

- **Describe a time you failed someone.** *(Answers may vary.)*

- **How did that person respond to you?** *(Answers may vary.)*

- **How do you feel about helping a homeless person?** *(it scares me, I'm very uncomfortable, I like the challenge, I think it'll be great to bless someone in this way, etc.)*

- **How do you think God wants you to respond to them?** *(with compassion, I'm not sure, I'm not sure He expects me to, like Jesus would, etc.)*

- **What is most difficult for you when trying to help or interact with a stranger who is very different than you?** *(I don't know what to say, I don't know how to respond if they say something weird or that doesn't make sense, I don't like that they are so dirty and don't smell good, I tend to blame them for their troubles, etc.)*

The Hand Bone's Connected to the...

Welcome summer by hosting a grill- and-game party for others.

BIBLE BASIS:
1 Corinthians 12:1–11

MEMORY VERSE:
There are different kinds of gifts, but the same Spirit. There are different kinds of service, but the same Lord.
1 Corinthians 12:4–5

BIBLE BACKGROUND

Do you suppose your foot is jealous because it has to stay down by your ankle and doesn't get to hang out on your wrist and do the seemingly more important things that hands do?

Of course not, that's silly.

Should your heart be proud because it's the pump that sends blood throughout your body and because it doesn't have to digest food as your stomach does?

Again, silly.

But this is just the kind of thing that was happening in the church in Corinth. The different members of the church body there were acting as if their individual spiritual gifts were in a pecking order of some kind. A person who served one way thought he was more valuable to the church than another person who served in a different way.

Paul is teaching the church at Corinth that everyone is gifted by the Spirit, for the Spirit. No one can decide what their own gifts will be, and so therefore, no one can take the credit for their gifts. And each gift is necessary. What would a hand do without the wrist to hold it onto the arm? What would a heart do without the stomach to receive the nutrients? How could a speaker of tongues serve the church in Corinth if there was no one to interpret the speech to others? Or how beneficial would it be to have a person sharing a message of knowledge if there was no one available to discern that his word was indeed from the Lord?

Each member of the Body of Christ has something to contribute, and each contribution is necessary and important to the proper function of the church. The gifts God has given us help us to work together so we can all be a part of His team.

PROJECT

Students will plan and host a "Welcome-to-Summer" grill party, inviting kids from school and the church neighborhood.

GOALS

- To allow students to work as a team, hosting a party for "outsiders"
- To offer a welcoming place for kids not usually a part of your group or church
- To help others get to know your students and perhaps foster new relationships

TEACHER'S TIPS

Explore with your students ways to identify and connect with other kids in your area whom they can invite. Help students consider inviting kids from school, community sports teams, or neighbors they know.

During preparation time, discuss with your students the various gifts that are present in your group. Find out which students are good with menu planning or making food, who is good at organizing, who feels comfortable greeting others and helping them feel welcome, and so forth. Once everyone discovers each other's gifts, lead them in brainstorming ways they can work together as a team to accomplish their mission.

Parents or other volunteers may be invited to help set up and man the grill(s), but as much as possible, allow the students to "run" the event. Offer suggestions regarding games and activities they can organize, efficient ways of preparing the food, and ideas for getting those they invited involved and having fun.

SUPPLY LIST

In class, during the planning stage:

- ☐ Invitations
- ☐ School directory and phone books for addresses
- ☐ Paper and pens for writing ideas and taking notes

For the day of the event:

- ☐ Grill(s)
- ☐ Food and condiments
- ☐ Drinks
- ☐ Sports equipment and supplies for outdoor games
- ☐ Tables and chairs

INSTRUCTIONS

In class, during the planning stage:

1. Determine the date, time, and location of your event.

2. Make up your guest list and create invitations. Encourage each student to invite at least one to two people who don't attend your group.

3. Plan the menu and get volunteers to bring various items.

4. Deliver or mail invitations.

On the day of the event:

1. Set up grills.

2. Set up tables for food.

3. As guests arrive, greet them and have games available to play.

4. Eat and have fun.

5. Clean up when finished, and leave area at least as nice as when you arrived.

PROJECT WRAP-UP!

Like a hand without a wrist, our gifts alone, without the gifts of others, aren't much good. God wants us to work together to accomplish His purpose.

- **How did you contribute to the planning and hosting of the event?** *(I planned the games, I helped figure out the best food to serve, etc.)*

- **In what way did your contribution use your unique abilities or gifts?** *(I'm good at helping new people feel comfortable, so I was in charge of greeting people; I'm good at organizing; so I set up the games, etc.)*

- **What do you find difficult about working with others?** *(I usually have different ideas than everyone else about how to do things, it's hard to let others help because I want to do it myself, etc.)*

- **What do you do best when you're working with a team?** *(I'm good at coming up with ways to combine different ideas, I can figure out how to do hard things, etc.)*

- **What other gifts do you recognize that are helpful for the Body of Christ?** *(I remember to pray for others, when I see a need I like to volunteer to help, etc.)*

Hope Full Pots

Use recycled materials to decorate a flower pot and offer hope.

BIBLE BASIS:
1 Corinthians 15:1–23

MEMORY VERSE:
If Christ has not been raised, your faith is futile; you are still in your sins.
1 Corinthians 15:17

BIBLE BACKGROUND

Think of something spectacular you have witnessed. It could be an amazing sporting event, a natural phenomenon like a tornado, a fire, or perhaps a daring rescue. You probably told people about what you saw, and those who were with you most likely told others as well.

When Jesus rose from the dead and appeared to over 500 people at once, they told others about it. But even though 500 people were witnesses, some still didn't believe. Can you imagine you and 500 other eyewitnesses telling about an unbelievable event and people saying, "Nah, I don't believe you"?

Without the event of Jesus' resurrection, there would be no basis for Christianity. It would be a waste of time, and we Christians, as Paul pointed out, would be pitiful. But it did happen. The whole foundation of Christianity is based on resurrection—of Jesus, of believers, and of God's whole creation, in the fullness of time, when the time is right (which God will decide).

Death came through Adam, as did the destruction of creation. But Jesus conquered death so *we* can one day conquer death. And one day, God's creation will also be restored to how it once was in the Garden of Eden. In Jesus' resurrection we find all that we hope for. It is Jesus who brings us new life.

PROJECT

Students will use recyclable paper products to decorate pots for Easter lilies, which will be given to senior ladies in the congregation or at a senior center.

GOALS

- To encourage students to "resurrect" old paper products to bless others in a creative manner
- To bless seniors with a part of God's creation that will remind them of Jesus' resurrection

TEACHER'S TIPS

Discuss with your students the significance of using recyclable products for your project. When a product is recycled and used again, it is, in a way, "brought back to life" for a new purpose. When Jesus died on the cross for us, He brought us back to life spiritually, and we now have a new purpose in Him.

The Easter lily is so named because it comes into bloom around Easter time, and is seen as a symbol of Christ's resurrection. Let the students know that if they have to use bulbs instead, they should tell the recipients to plant them at any time. They can even offer to plant them for the recipient.

As you decide who you want to give your Hope Full Pots to, consider the number of senior ladies in your congregation. If there are too few or too many in relation to your number of students, it may be better to choose a senior center to deliver them to.

SUPPLY LIST

- ☐ 6" clay/terra-cotta flowerpots
- ☐ Variety of used paper products (newspaper, thin cardboard, paper bags, magazines, etc.)
- ☐ Rubber cement or tacky craft glue
- ☐ Scissors
- ☐ Pencils
- ☐ Permanent markers (variety of colors)
- ☐ Clear acrylic paint
- ☐ Paintbrushes (1 per student)
- ☐ Small Easter lily or bulb, if plants are not available (1 per student)
- ☐ Potting soil and spades (if lilies are available)
- ☐ Tulle (any color) and ribbon (if using bulbs)
- ☐ Damp cloths or paper towels

do ahead Purchase either Easter lilies or their bulbs, if the lilies are not in season. Have one lily or bulb available for each student. Have students bring a variety of paper products to class (see Supply List for ideas). Decide who will be the recipients for your flowerpots. If you choose a senior center, ask the center for the best day and time to deliver the pots, then make arrangements for delivery.

INSTRUCTIONS

1. Wipe down the pots with damp cloths.

2. Have students select the paper products they want to use to decorate their pots. They should use several different varieties.

3. Using pencils, have students draw cross shapes on the paper they selected. Crosses should be between 1" and 4" tall and can be various sizes.

4. Cut crosses from paper.

5. Spread a thin layer of glue onto back of crosses, then glue onto the pot randomly or in a pattern. Crosses should decorate the entire circumference of the pot.

6. Using permanent markers, add a resurrection message to the top rim of the pot. Suggestions include: "He is alive!," "Jesus' resurrection gives us hope," etc.

7. For lilies, use a spade to fill pot ⅓ to ½ full with potting soil, place root ball of lily into soil, then fill remainder of pot with soil. For bulbs, wrap bulb in 3" square of tulle, then tie with ribbon. Place wrapped bulb inside pot.

8. Clean off any dirt from the outside of the pot.

9. Brush a thin layer of clear acrylic paint over the entire pot to protect the crosses and add shine. Allow to dry before touching. (Paint in an open or well-ventilated area.)

10. Deliver the pots to senior ladies in your congregation or to a designated senior center, letting recipients know that Easter lilies, as well as recycled paper, were chosen to remind them of Jesus' resurrection.

PROJECT WRAP-UP!

Jesus' resurrection means new life for us. It also means that we can have hope for an eternity spent with God in heaven. Since we have this hope in our hearts, we should do all we can to encourage others, letting them know that Jesus has provided hope for their future too.

- **What does Jesus' resurrection mean to you?** *(that I can go to heaven when I die if I ask Him into my heart, that I don't have to be afraid of death, that He truly is the Son of God, etc.)*

- **Why is it important to have hope for your eternal future?** *(so I can look forward to something beyond this life, it helps me stay focused on the things of God instead of the bad things I sometimes have to deal with, etc.)*

- **Discuss a time when you were able to share with others something about Jesus' resurrection or eternity.** *(Answers may vary.)*

- **What are some other ideas that might be used to remind yourself or others of Jesus' resurrection?** *(Answers may vary.)*

Stand Firm

BIBLE BASIS:
Ephesians 6:10–17

MEMORY VERSE:
Let the word of Christ dwell in you richly as you teach and admonish one another with all wisdom. Colossians 3:16

BIBLE BACKGROUND

If you've played hockey or soccer, you know the importance of protective gear. If you've ever been lobbed in the head by a high, wild pitch, you know how essential a batting helmet is. Would you ever consider sparring without a mouth guard? Not if you'd like to keep your teeth. Protective gear is vital when you go against an opponent.

Paul recognized all too well the need for protection. He knew he was a big target for the enemy who was trying hard to bring him down. Paul had to be on guard and have himself fully prepared in order to withstand the enemy. Imagine trying to play soccer without shin guards, or being a hockey goalie and guarding the net without your facemask on. Not only could you get hurt, but also you'd probably play a lot more timidly knowing how vulnerable you were. You'd back off and not stand firm, because to get a hockey puck in the nose is absolutely no fun!

Getting an attack from the evil one is painful too. But we *can* withstand it if we are properly prepared. Paul instructed us to put on the full armor of God. We are to be strong in the Lord and rest in His mighty power. We do that by preparing ourselves through prayer, through a knowledge and understanding of God's Word, by embracing His truth and righteousness, by walking in peace and faith, and by standing on the assurance of our salvation—knowing that we are eternally safe with God.

So ready yourself. Put on your shin guards, your facemask, and your batting helmet. Sink your teeth into your mouth guard. And stand firm!

PROJECT

Students will send notes of support and encouragement to missionaries that include specially chosen Scripture verses to help them be better equipped for the challenges they face on the mission field.

GOALS

- To allow students to stand firm alongside those serving in missions against the attacks of the enemy
- To help students learn and practice using Bible concordances to find particular Scripture verses
- To provide encouragement to missionaries

TEACHER'S TIPS

Help the students identify with the missionaries to whom they are writing by providing information about them, where they serve, and some details about their situations. Consider exploring with them the social, economic, and political challenges that citizens face in the missionaries' regions of service. Talk about any religious oppression or persecution in their area.

Then discuss how best the students can support the missionaries through their notes containing Scripture verses. Remind them that the sword of the Spirit is the Word of God, and it has power over Satan. Assist them in finding verses that will speak to and encourage the missionaries. Help them understand that even if the missionaries have known the verses well, the verses may be just what they need at the time they receive them.

SUPPLY LIST

- ☐ Stationery or note cards
- ☐ Envelopes
- ☐ 3" x 5" index cards
- ☐ Pens
- ☐ Bibles
- ☐ Bible concordances for every few students
- ☐ Computer or laptop, if available, for online Bible concordance
- ☐ Names and addresses of missionaries

 **do ahead** Collect names and mailing information for missionaries supported by or in relationship with your church. Gather Bible concordances for students to use in class. Try to find different kinds, both topical and keyword, and have online resource information available, such as www.biblegateway.com.

INSTRUCTIONS

1. Learn about and discuss the missionaries to whom the letters will be written. Pray for them.

2. Use Bible concordances to choose Bible verses to include with the letters.

3. Write the verses and references on 3" x 5" cards.

4. Compose short letters of support and encouragement to the missionaries, explaining your purpose of sending them the Word of God to equip them for their work.

5. Enclose letters with 3" x 5" cards in envelopes.

6. Address envelopes.

7. Mail.

PROJECT WRAP-UP!

God gives us what we need to persevere in the challenges we face. If we read, study, and learn His Scripture, we will strengthen our protective gear—the armor of God—to help us fight against the schemes of the enemy.

- **What spiritual challenge(s) do you face?** *(fear, need to control, depression, discouragement, a certain temptation, etc.)*

- **What are your favorite verses you use to battle against your challenge(s)?** *(Answers will vary.)*

- **Can you describe a time you faced a spiritual battle and how you stood firm, or perhaps didn't because you weren't equipped—in other words, weren't wearing the full armor of God?** *(Answers may vary.)*

- **What happens when you don't have the necessary Scripture available when you face challenges?** *(I try to resist on my own strength, my fear grows, it's harder to stay strong, etc.)*

- **What can you do to better prepare for future challenges?** *(spend regular time reading the Bible, memorize verses that I know can help me, learn to use a Bible concordance, etc.)*

- **What new verses did you find that were meaningful to you as you chose verses to send to the missionaries?** *(Answers will vary.)*

How's Your Serve? SCRIPTURE AND TOPIC INDEX

The following index allows you to use this book with any curriculum.

Simply find the Scripture your lesson is based on or the topic you are teaching.

Scripture	Topic	Page
Genesis 1:26–28	God's love, Self-image	6
Genesis 2:7	God's love, Self-image	6
Genesis 2:18–23	Building relationships, Senior citizens	10
Genesis 4:1–16	Mercy	14
Genesis 11:1–9	Humility, Pride	18
Genesis 14:14—15:1	Stewardship	22
Genesis 22:1–12	Faith, Sacrifice, Trust, Homeless/Needy	26
Genesis 29:13–30	Trust, Building relationships	30
Genesis 31:38–45	Trust, Building relationships	30
Genesis 31:51–53	Trust, Building relationships	30
Genesis 45:1–11	Forgiveness, Peace, Past experiences	34
Jeremiah 1:1–7	Strength in God, Service	38
Jeremiah 7:1–7	Strength in God, Service	38
Matthew 4:1–11	God's Word, Temptation	42
Matthew 5:38–48	Kindness	78
Matthew 9:9–13	Faith, Service, Cliques	46
Matthew 14:22–23a	Prayer	50
Mark 2:1–12	Forgiveness, Homeless/Needy	54
Mark 10:17–21	Security	58
Mark 14:32–36	Prayer	50
Luke 1:26–38	Miracles, Homeless/Needy	62
Luke 2:1–20	Christmas, Proclaiming the Good News	66
Luke 3:7–14	Repentance, Building relationships, Cliques	70
Luke 4:16–22	Service, Homeless/Needy	74
Luke 6:12–16	Prayer	50
Luke 9:51–56	Kindness	78
Luke 17:11–19	Thankfulness/Gratitude, Military	82
Luke 18:9–14	Humility, Pride, Thankfulness/Gratitude	86
John 17:1, 6–9, 13-15, 20-24	Prayer	90
John 21:3–17	Grace, Homeless/Needy	94
1 Corinthians 12:1–11	Spiritual gifts, Body of Christ	98
1 Corinthians 15:1–23	Resurrection, Hope	102
Ephesians 6:10–17	Armor of God	106

How's Your Serve? CORRELATION CHART

Each activity correlates to a Unit and Lesson in the curriculum lines shown below.

For further help on how to use the chart see page 5.

Title	Page	Scripture Reference	David C. Cook BIL LifeLINKS to God College Press Reformation Press Wesley Anglican	Echoes The Cross
And It Was Very Good	6	Genesis 1:26–28; 2:7	Unit 1, Lesson 2	Unit 1, Lesson 2
Best Friends Forever	10	Genesis 2:18–23	Unit 1, Lesson 4	Unit 1, Lesson 4
Mercy Me	14	Genesis 4:1–16	Unit 2, Lesson 6	Unit 2, Lesson 6
I've Fallen, and I Can't Get Up	18	Genesis 11:1–9	Unit 2, Lesson 8	Unit 2, Lesson 8
A Penny for Our Pots?	22	Genesis 14:14—15:1	Unit 3, Lesson 10	Unit 3, Lesson 10
Trust in Him	26	Genesis 22:1–12	Unit 3, Lesson 12	Unit 3, Lesson 12
Possibly the Impossible	62	Luke 1:26–38	Unit 4, Lesson 1	Unit 4, Lesson 1
Shout It Out	66	Luke 2:1–20	Unit 4, Lesson 3	Unit 4, Lesson 4
Got Any Change?	70	Luke 3:7–14	Unit 5, Lesson 5	Unit 5, Lesson 5
Man Does Not Live by Cupcakes Alone	42	Matthew 4:1–11	Unit 5, Lesson 7	Unit 5, Lesson 7
Mission Possible	74	Luke 4:16–22	Unit 5, Lesson 9	Unit 5, Lesson 9
"BE MINE," Says Jesus	46	Matthew 9:9–13	Unit 6, Lesson 11	Unit 6, Lesson 11
Thank God!	82	Luke 17:11–19	Unit 6, Lesson 13	Unit 6, Lesson 13
A Can Can Cheer	54	Mark 2:1–12	Unit 7, Lesson 2	Unit 7, Lesson 2
Let 'Em Have It!	78	Luke 9:51–56; Matthew 5:38–48	Unit 7, Lesson 4	Unit 7, Lesson 4
Let's Do Lunch	94	John 21:3–17	Unit 8, Lesson 6	Unit 8, Lesson 6
Hang On	58	Mark 10:17–21	Unit 8, Lesson 8	Unit 7, Lesson 8
Would I Lie to You?	30	Genesis 29:13–30; 31:38–45, 51–53	Unit 9, Lesson 10	Unit 9, Lesson 10
Piece of Peace	34	Genesis 45:1–11	Unit 9, Lesson 12	Unit 9, Lesson 12
The Hand Bone's Connected to the …	98	1 Corinthians 12:1–11	Unit 10, Lesson 1	Unit 10, Lesson 1
Hope Full Pots	102	1 Corinthians 15:1–23	Unit 10, Lesson 3	Unit 10, Lesson 3
Fast: Food	50	Matthew 14:22–23a; Mark 14:32–36; Luke 6:12–16	Unit 11, Lesson 5	Unit 11, Lesson 5
It's the Heart That Matters	86	Luke 18:9–14	Unit 11, Lesson 7	Unit 11, Lesson 7
i m praying 4 u	90	John 17:1, 6–9, 13–15, 20–24	Unit 11, Lesson 9	Unit 11, Lesson 9
… But He Is Strong	38	Jeremiah 1:1–7; 7:1–7	Unit 12, Lesson 11	Unit 12, Lesson 11
Stand Firm	106	Ephesians 6:10–17	Unit 12, Lesson 13	Unit 12, Lesson 13